Andrew Clitherow is Director ... Blackburn and a Canon Res... edral. Prior to taking up his ... ...ent, he was the vicar of a busy suburban p... ...sh in Lancaster where he worked with others to set up a Retreat and Renewal Centre for those living in Urban Priority Areas.

Renewing Faith in Ordained Ministry

New Hope for Tired Clergy

Written for those in ordained ministry and
for anyone seeking a renewed understanding
of this ministry today

Andrew Clitherow

First published in Great Britain in 2004 by
SPCK
Holy Trinity Church
Marylebone Road
London NW1 4DU

British Library Cataloguing-in-Publication Data
A catalogue record for this book is available
from the British Library

ISBN 0-281-05643-9

1 3 5 7 9 10 8 6 4 2

Typeset by Avocet Typeset, Chilton, Aylesbury, Bucks
Printed in Great Britain by Bookmarque Ltd, Croydon, Surrey

CONTENTS

For
my parents,
Dick and Diana

With thanks to Saskia Barnden for reading the draft text and for her helpful advice and comments. With thanks also to my wife, Rebekah, for her love, support and spiritual insight.

INTRODUCTION

This book originated from a series of three addresses I was invited to give at the Durham Diocese Clergy Summer School held at Ushaw College in July of 2003.

I should like therefore to express my sincere thanks to Canon Adrian Dorber and the Revd Dr Nicholas Chamberlain for their kind invitation to speak at the conference and to Bishop John Pritchard for his comments and support at the time.

My aim was to speak about how clergy might be able to find ways to reflect on the nature of their calling and ministry when both the church and the society it seeks to serve are going through a time of change and transition. Therefore I subtitled my talks 'hanging on to vocational holiness at a time of death and resurrection'.

Like many clergy, I guess, I am frequently shocked by the paucity of my spiritual life and dismayed at the lack of prayerful love in my day-to-day life. As a young priest I had ideals and dreams. Now I have to fight against a creeping cynicism and sense of nightmare.

I take comfort, however, that there was a certain arrogance about my youthful optimism, some of which at least has now gone. Nowadays I am more likely to serve others from a place of weakness where I hope God is strong rather than from a position of perceived, yet misunderstood, strength. I hope I have in some small degree exchanged an abuse of clerical power for the more gentle approach of the servant.

This making and remaking of the minister's life is both demanding and intrinsic to the role of those who find themselves called to positions of leadership within the church. It can be difficult to handle positively. It means that we have to be open to re-examine and even on occasions to redefine our understanding of ministry and prayer. In addition, from time to time we should look again at our understanding of the way the Spirit of God functions within the myriad creative processes of life that are themselves subject to constant change.

Add to this process of change a proliferation of approaches to the gospel, each claiming its own authenticity, and a society that makes little sense of the religion we appear to be peddling, and we can end up feeling that we are in a failing institution where ministry is largely defined as managing decline.

It is not all bad news, of course. In some areas there are signs of significant growth where the church is developing and leading people to a living faith in God. Such stories should be told and celebrated and yet, to be brutally frank, the church as a whole still makes little meaningful contact with the vast majority of people in our society today.

This book maintains that however we change what we do and how we do it – and at present there is a plethora of 'how to be a new and vibrant church in touch with real life' books – holding on to a sense of the holiness of Christian life and ministry remains of central importance.

But what do we make of this holiness – or humility – in a changing church? Do our concepts of holiness and humility change? Should we re-brand them in our sometimes pathetic attempts to market the gospel? Or is there a core structure to these things that was there at the beginning of the faith of our ancestors, and that we have overlooked today?

I propose that it is extremely important that we step back and look at ourselves apart from the models of church and ministry that are defined by financial necessity. By looking at everything with some faithful detachment, we can begin to rediscover our vocation in a new and exciting way. And this will help us to re-engage with the church and society.

Here humility and faith are not confined within the walls of a building used for a few hours a week by a handful of people. Nor are they restricted to a building that now operates as a worship centre, parish hall, youth centre and so on depending on what time of which day of the week you happen to turn up. Instead, they are to be rediscovered in the very midst of human relationships; wherever and however we try to live them out.

So this book is absolutely not just another one principally concerned with structures. It offers no help to anyone who wants a blueprint of how we can quality control the gospel or develop effective management. And I suspect it will make little sense to those who feel threatened by any kind of radical love that may make them look at themselves and their religion from a different perspective.

Instead, this book is about relationships. It is about how relationships can make sense or non-sense of us at different stages in our journey of faith. It is about the relationship that those called to Christian ministry have with themselves, with others and with God.

It is about how these relationships can become strained and even confused in today's changing world. It is about how we can understand that relationships need to develop and grow if we as ministers are to fulfil our potential. It is about how God calls us to develop our relationship of love with him and with the world he has created.

It is about going deeper into our relationship with ourselves and understanding better our relationships with others. It is about the celebration of a journey of hope and new life over against cynicism and nightmare.

Above all, it is about the joyful freedom that Christ-centred humility and love can give.

In the pages that follow, I have approached the principal theme from three different perspectives. These run through all three chapters and a short introduction about what these three themes are should help the reader to make the most of the structure that I have adopted.

First, I am going to refer to the story of Jacob from the Old Testament. Not an obvious choice, you might think, for a study of ministry today. But while the vast differences between his story and ours are very evident, there are similarities in his journey of faith that are of significant interest as we try and come to terms with our changing circumstances. Not least in the way we struggle to make sense of tradition in a very changing world while trying to hang on to our identity. So this understanding of the journey of Jacob is different from the one we most commonly hear about.

In turn, I shall refer to Jacob's sudden departure from his family home, his dream at Bethel, his life with his father-in-law, his struggle with the angel and his reconciliation with his brother Esau.

Second, I want to suggest that if we are to revisit our understanding of our vocation, our identity as priests and our call to become holy people, we need to understand our own reactions to what we are going through.

One of the most effective ways of doing this is to be found in the realization that what we are experiencing is not simply a loss of identity or direction or a crisis of faith. In fact, the emotions that we often display are identical to those normally found in the grieving process.

Identifying these as such means that we can move on from being subject to mood swings and the feelings of emptiness and powerlessness that they can bring, to regain some kind of control over our identity and purpose.

So, alongside the journey of Jacob, I will be looking at the four tasks of the grieving process which are: (i) accepting that our loss is a reality; (ii) entering into the emotions of grief; (iii) acquiring new skills; and (iv) reinvesting our energy in new ways.[1]

The third question that will run through this text will be how we might try and describe the way in which we seek to understand Christian holiness in terms of personal humility. In order to fulfil our potential as ministers we have to become the people God has called us to be.

It can hardly be said that humility is the hallmark of much of what we do. Humility has, of course, nothing to do with a spineless form of spirituality that reduces Christians to the status of faithful lapdogs whose purpose is to massage the egotistical ambitions of Western consumerism.

As we shall see, Christian humility – properly understood – grounds the faith of the individual and the worshipping community firmly within the processes of the love of God within all of creation.

Finally, I would suggest that in order to make the most of what follows, the reader should be prepared to embark on a journey in the company of Jacob. It appears that while much is written about how we might 'be church' in a different way, not much has been said about how the gospel asks us to become 'ourselves' in a different way.

This becoming begins with our experience of relationships. It does not start from those religious definitions that begin not with ourselves but, rather unhelpfully, with who we think we ought to be. For when we use our religion to place ourselves in an orbit around an imagined point somewhere distant and distinct from the human condition, our spiritual development is inevitably restricted to recurrent circles rather than any kind of evolutionary development.

So this is a journey of faith and love. It may therefore at times be untidy, unsettling and demanding. But above all it should be exciting and dynamic.

Andrew Clitherow

1

CALLED OR CULLED?

Jacob and tradition

Let us begin with the story of Jacob. We join it when, as a young man, Jacob's life is in danger. Having lost to Jacob both his birthright and the blessing of his father – which was his right as the elder son – Esau has decided that he has had enough of his brother and now plans to kill him.

> *Now Esau hated Jacob because of the blessing with which his father had blessed him, and Esau said to himself, 'The days of mourning for my father are approaching; then I will kill my brother Jacob.' But the words of her elder son Esau were told to Rebekah; so she sent and called her younger son Jacob and said to him, 'Your brother Esau is consoling himself by planning to kill you. Now therefore, my son, obey my voice; flee at once to my brother Laban in Haran, and stay with him for a while, until your brother's fury turns away – until your brother's anger against you turns away, and he forgets what you have done to him; then I will send, and bring you back from there. Why should I lose both of you in one day?'*
> (Genesis 27.41–45)

It has been traditional to understand Jacob as being deceitful, headstrong, impatient and very ambitious. He has no time for playing second fiddle to his brother. He is the bad

7

guy who turns out good in the end. He lies his way through his upbringing, eventually running away in fear of his life. Then through a number of misfortunes he comes to his senses. In the end he makes his peace with God. As a result he is reconciled to his brother and settles down to watch his children become the fathers of the tribes of the Israelite people. By all accounts Esau loses and Jacob wins.

This after all was Jacob's destiny. Even at birth Jacob, the younger of the two, was delivered into the world while holding on to his brother's ankle, as if to hold him back.

There's more than a passing similarity here to the story Jesus told about two sons. The older one stays at home and exemplifies a traditional loyalty to his father. The younger one – unhappy and impatient – seizes his inheritance early and goes off to enjoy the best of life's luxuries and excesses. Eventually he returns, penitent and seeking forgiveness. His father welcomes him back, treating him with a generosity that the elder son had not known (Luke 15.11–32).

The last shall be first and all that. Toiling in the heat of the day and watching the latecomers who have been pleasing themselves come in ahead or at least alongside us. This is not good news when you are exhausted, you've given your all and somehow the deal you thought you had with God has fallen through.

At times it is very hard to cope with the pressures of ministry when a different set of rules seems to apply to those who have given up far less than we think we have. It is difficult to avoid cynicism when some of those who have voted against a meagre pay increase for parochial clergy drive home from the meeting in cars that cost the equivalent of two years' stipend.

Maybe we misunderstood the agreement. Perhaps we have been working on false premises. Or maybe we are just tired and have lost sight of the kingdom.

But could God really be so unfair? Poor old Esau. He gets

no special praise while his ambitious brother breaks all the rules and gets to be given the name by which the nation of the covenant will be known.

Is this really the way God's love works? Are we simply dealing with the history of an emerging nation? Or do we have to be permanently inhibited by an unhelpful Bible tradition?

Priesthood and change

I want to suggest, however, that there is another, quite different and altogether more helpful allegorical interpretation of the story of Jacob.

This will help us as we try and come to terms with a tradition of faith and our membership of a church that no longer seems to command the respect it once did. I hope it will also help us come to terms with the loss of a traditional understanding of the role of the parish priest. And, as we shall see, this interpretation will help us deal with *our* dreams and ambition.

I was ordained some twenty-five years ago. Then, I naively thought that the nature and practice of priesthood within the Church of England was one of those matters about which there was general agreement. I thought that everyone had a more or less similar understanding of what we were about.

While team ministry was on the increase, even within those teams there seemed to be at least a general agreement about models of ministry. Ordained ministry was primarily stipendiary and centred upon the sacraments, pastoral care and spiritual leadership.

Today there is such diversity of role and such diversification of function that it is no longer straightforward to define the role of the priest. More often than not, it depends upon where you are and also who you are.

Stipendiary ministry is becoming less exclusive in a number of ways. And recent years have seen a celebration of the work of those who are ministers in secular employment, non-stipendiaries (who can be incumbents and area deans) and also ordained local ministers.

This is not to mention the various chaplaincies, most of which have been in existence a lot longer than twenty-five years. School, hospital, prison and armed forces posts – misunderstood by some in the past as somehow inferior to full-time parish work – are held in greater esteem today.

We have yet to work out the full implications of some of these ministries as they develop. NSMs frequently feel left out on a limb and while one diocese may confine its OLMs to their parishes, another may allow them to minister in other parishes for a fixed number of Sundays a year. For some these are exciting developments but for others they are confusing and frightening.

Inevitably, I suppose, secular management systems have been adopted to cope with these developments and the diversification of discipleship. Diocesan bishops more often than not are encouraged to combine being spiritual leaders with being senior executive officers. Suffragan bishops and archdeacons face similar pressures. And most recently area deans are becoming area managers for parish clergy, in some circumstances being responsible for conducting their annual appraisal.

For better or for worse – whichever way you look at it – times are changing and ministry today is quite different from what it was even twenty-five years ago.

Sometimes we can feel that as we use secular management models we are at the same time being seduced by the culture of the marketplace. So we often speak less in terms of parishioners and more about customers, less about spiritual discipline and more about value for money, less about repentance and more about marketing. And there are even those who think we should quality control the gospel.

What is more, the place of the parish priest within the worshipping community and the wider community is changing. We are now increasingly encouraged to develop the vocation and ministries of the laity and to develop what we call ministry teams to work alongside and to complement the ministry of the priest and PCC. The parish priest is the one who leads and nurtures the team leaders and is likely therefore to be even further removed from the shop floor.

In general terms it appears that most parishes prefer to have the incumbent as the senior manager of the set-up while at the same time retaining all the traditional expectations of the role.

But some feel that within legal parameters they want to free their clergy of all that lay people can do. They want their priests to concentrate on their spiritual life, to become people of prayer and to spend their time alongside others in the wider community, on the margins of parish life during the week. They want the clergy to be about ministry in the world – going where the church is not – and at the weekends to be in and about church, mediating, interceding and presiding in prayer and sacrament.

In addition to the change in role, ordained ministers – both men and women – who live in parsonage houses find themselves under all sorts of pressure today. Nowadays you and your family can feel under siege at times and almost unable to maintain any real quality of life for yourselves because people are forever on the front doorstep and the phone never stops and when it does 'they' are still trying to get at you silently and stealthily by email.

You might think this is unduly pessimistic and that there are great joys in growth and development that should be outlined here as well. I have avoided those because I want first of all to lance the boil of latent discontent among many who are in ordained ministry today. So while I am concentrating first on some of the frustrations of ministry, I am by no means suggesting that parish ministry is all bad news. But it is under new and increasing pressure and there is little sign of it abating.

I still firmly believe that being based in a parish is probably the best and most rewarding ministry in the church. But the numbers of clergy who suffer from stress – and their families who suffer from the effects of stress – are increasing faster than we can come up with either ways of redefining our ministry or effective means of protecting ourselves and managing the pressures.

Managing other people's expectations of clergy has always been difficult but it seems as if the expectations are even greater and more unreasonable than ever. Add to this the mountains of paperwork that seem to come at us from all directions, increasing bureaucracy and the pressure of the parish share, and it is small wonder that we struggle at times to make sense of it all.

So it will come as no surprise when I say that it can be very difficult – over the years – to hold on to the love of Christ in this ever-changing situation and indeed to hold on to our identity as priests, too.

When we have been encouraged to subcontract another part of our ministry to others who are not ordained, while under pressure to take on roles of management for which we have never been trained and also worrying whether or not the institution will survive much longer, we can end up asking the question, 'What we are here for?' What is our role? How do we handle this identity crisis? We were called to be ordained ministers within the church yet we feel that many priests are being culled because the church can no longer afford us. Moreover, the institution is finding it increasingly difficult to justify a role for us.

Recently I led a parish weekend where one of the exercises was to divide into groups and devise a different structure for church community in contrast to the traditional set-up that we currently have. In all the group submissions not one of them mentioned the role of the stipendiary incumbent. This was all the more extraordinary as the ministry of the parish priest – a godly and deeply spiritual person – was very highly thought of. Perhaps the results indicated how much the people took him for granted. Or maybe they wanted him to earn his living – like St Paul – and become today's equivalent of a tent-maker.

The love which we pray for and encourage others to live by, the love we hope to model to others, the love that can alone bring peace to a society – and indeed a world – that is ill at ease with itself seems easily lost beneath agendas for change. These agendas appear to acquire an immense power of their own to which our simple desire to pursue the paths of prayer and love become subject and subordinate. Agendas for change driven through diocesan synods – as if to bring in the kingdom next week – can leave us feeling dizzy and disorientated.

When the desire to love is suppressed by outside forces, we can feel almost helpless in the face of our emotions when they are finally released. In a very different setting, Iris Murdoch provides a vivid description of how we can be left feeling as if we are 'spinning like a top, whirling away into invisibility . . . kitten-limbed and crucified by centrifugal force'.[1] Sometimes, when the life of parish and diocese and a society we no longer really understand forces us to deny the love of the gospel and of Jesus Christ that lies at the heart of our vocation, we can end up feeling just like this.

Society and change

So far we have looked at some of the changes that face us within the church. But, of course, many of these have been brought about because of the changes in society. For far longer than it should have, the church continued to believe that it was at the centre of society. Once the life of the community revolved around the life of the church. Once the ordained minister had a clearly defined role as social worker, spiritual guide, pastoral shepherd, local politician and academic . . . the list goes on.

Now we suddenly discover that society has moved on – actually it moved on some time ago – and it has left us behind. The church still comes into its own in times of crisis when people will flock to and fill our churches and cathedrals; as we saw following the tragic murder of two little girls – Jessica Chapman and Holly Wells – in Soham, Cambridgeshire. But for most of the time, the church has been relegated to the status of part-time activity in competition with others. Its uniqueness has disappeared. In a twenty-four-seven society, Sunday has become increasingly for work or trips to the supermarket and garden centre and for precious family time at home rather than a time of sabbatical and spiritual sustenance centred on the sacraments of the church.

One of the reasons why we may feel 'kitten-limbed and crucified' is that we just cannot cope with the rate at which all these changes are taking place. No generation before us has had to cope with such an accelerated rate of change. As far back as 1969, Alvin and Heidi Toffler were writing about the tensions associated with 'the premature arrival of the future' describing these as 'future shock'. They defined this 'future shock' as 'the shattering stress and disorientation that we induce in individuals by subjecting them to too much change in too short a time . . . it arises from the superimposition of a new culture on an old one'.[2]

For most of us the church – by definition – invests enormous amounts of energy in, and attaches great importance to, the past as a context for the present. As an institution the church's resistance to sudden change has been at various times both a sign of its great strength and also of its weakness.

On the one hand, we might want to say that the morality of the secular world is in some ways way ahead of the morality of the church. Instead of leading the way in the campaign for women's rights and the tolerance of differences in sexual orientation, the church sometimes struggles to catch up with the progressive understanding of human nature and tolerance of difference in society.

Conversely, we might want to argue that when the church refuses to be swayed by this and that latest fashion and philosophy it shows itself to be grounded in ultimate truth. Here the community of faith lives within the context of the redemptive history of God as passed down to us through Old and New Covenants and the tradition of the church. So future shock for those who have such a complex relationship with the past is doubly difficult to handle, for it is less than clear when our interpretation renders us obedient or disobedient to the will of God.

Salvation and myself

Moral relativism within the church – as well as outside – means that our salvation is no longer defined by creeds and councils. It now belongs to individuals exercising their own rights and responsibilities.

As we take on this responsibility ourselves in the absence of any concept of ultimate authority in the traditional sense, one person's strength can easily be another person's weakness. In other words, in this freedom to live by love rather than law, it is not always clear what is moral strength or weakness. Whereas the law exerts some kind of guiding restraint on human nature, the less well-defined processes of love sometimes give us more freedom than we can cope with.

But if traditional structures of ecclesiastical order are disappearing – and many would say that it was about time they did – can we reduce our ability or inability to react positively to change and the demands of love, to the influences of our background, upbringing and personal preference?

Are theological standpoint and liturgical preference really determined by our Myers Briggs personality indicators? Is our understanding of the theology of holy orders really to do with our understanding or lack of understanding of ourselves? Is the central core of the Christian life really biologically based in a cluster of religious genes or is there more to us than this?

One of the results of this 'future shock' and the uncertainty of identity and role is that we strike out at others. We need to attach blame to someone. Who was it that got us into this mess? Why didn't they see it coming? Why are their attempts to get us out of it so pathetic? Those on this list will include the Church Commissioners, the Archbishop's Council, bishops generally, the cathedral and the diocese.

Such feelings as these are natural reactions when we are insecure and afraid. But while they can preserve a kind of emotional equilibrium in us, if they are not understood for what they are, they can be very destructive. For when they are misunderstood they can manufacture a blame culture that means that we can avoid any new inward investment in ourselves. We find a way to blame others for our loss of faith because we are afraid to face up to what we have lost.

So we feel anger, resentment, fear and confusion either because we are reluctant to face reality or because we have been so taken by surprise by the fairly recent turn of events that indicate terminal decline that we remain in a state of shock.

Or perhaps our unhappiness is unmanageable because

we haven't realized what it is exactly that we are living through.

Waking up to what is going on

We may feel that much of what we are doing as parish priests is managing decline. As we trace the decline in church membership over the last forty years or so, we can draw a graph by which we can put a date on the demise of this institution if current trends persist.

But we can feel faithless when we think like this. We feel we should live by hope. One day God will come to the rescue of his church. We just have to come up with the right formula to make that possible.

The result of this self-imposed guilt is that we can end up in denial. We refuse to accept that something we love and cherish, something we have given our lives to and sacrificed ourselves for, is in fact terminally ill. We cannot accept it because we have not lost all faith and therefore hope. After all, we are supposed to be an Easter people, or so they keep telling us and we keep telling others.

Some ten years ago, when I was a parish priest in Lancaster, my marriage fell apart. In the end my wife and I with great reluctance and no little anguish decided it would be best for everyone if we were to separate. So with our two young children she moved out of the vicarage and set up home elsewhere.

This was without doubt the most shattering experience of my life. The sense of loss was dreadful. The separation from those to whom I was devoted brought a pain I would not wish on anyone.

I continued with my ministry, yet inside I was empty and living a dream that all too often became a nightmare.

I was not unfamiliar with suffering nor was I a stranger to death and grief, yet it was a while before I realized what it was that I was going through. All the emotions I was experiencing were those normally associated with the grieving process. I had anticipated the feelings of devastation but it had not crossed my mind that grief was to be my closest companion in the coming months and years of readjustment that lay ahead.

However, once I had identified that I was going through a grieving process, I began to understand my feelings. This provided me with the knowledge I needed to manage my emotions in a proactive manner rather than reacting to them all the time in a self-inhibiting and limiting way. So I found ways to cope with the pain.

In a similar manner, the feelings that many clergy have today concerning the current state of the church are associated with grief. But while grief is often the source of low morale, a sense of helplessness and a reactive and rather depressing outlook on ministry, it is very seldom recognized or understood.

While God has not yet moved out of our house and taken the church with him, we are reacting now to their impending departure at some as yet undetermined time in the future. We are mourning the loss of a relationship of love to which we have given our lives at a considerable cost to ourselves, not only financial but also emotional and sometimes spiritual. We have been devoted in our service of Jesus Christ and our fellow human beings and we sense that so much of what we cherished and has given us meaning and even identity is being taken away from us – is dying – and we are powerless to do anything about it.

One of the ways, therefore, in which we can become empowered again is to face up to why we are feeling as we do. To recognize our grief. To own it and even make friends with it so that we can handle it and work through it.

So often our faith can be a way by which we deny what we are feeling because we think for some reason or other we shouldn't feel as we do. But ours is not a gospel of denial but of truth. We cannot expect to have 'life in all its fullness' if we cannot face up to reality. So we have no alternative but to face up to the pain we suffer when love goes wrong. And if we approach this situation using our knowledge of the grieving process and how best to handle it, we can find a way to accommodate the pain without allowing it to destroy our hope that love will triumph in the future.

There are at least four tasks that we perform as we work with grief. They don't come in any set order and we may experience any one of them more than once. But at some time or other we are likely to be aware of all four. And it is likely that we shall need to work through all four tasks in order to handle our feelings effectively.

Accepting loss as a reality

The first task of grief I want to look at is the importance of accepting our loss as a reality. It seems to me that when facing the challenges of ministry today we may simply want to go on as if nothing is happening. We may insist on continuing with the models of ministry and the understanding of God that we have always used. Shying away from necessary change, we can pretend that we will cope with whatever comes without facing up to any of the real pain.

Maybe, however, it is not a denial of our vocation to face up to the fact that the church, which we know and love, is dying. But like someone who is terminally ill, it can look little different from the way it did before when we felt that everything was all right. It may look a little gaunt at times but all the limbs are still working to some degree and outward appearances give the impression of business pretty much as usual.

One of the consequences of this denial is that we carry on

as normal instead of preparing for the next stage because we refuse to accept that this illness is really terminal.

Much of our reaction to the crisis in the church at present is seen in terms of expending vast amounts of time and energy in trying to keep alive what will inevitably die. Facing a dearth of vocations we adopt a 'go out and grab 'em' approach in order to keep the existing structures going.

Why can we not face up instead to the painful prospect that it may well be within God's plan for his church that the present institution as it is – which has been highly effective in its day – needs now to die so that a new and reinvigorated church may take its place? Why can we not face up to the fact that it may be within the will of God that in the church of the future there will be fewer priests?

This analysis might sound unbearably morbid but facing death can also be the point from which we can begin to find a kind of peace about what is happening. Instead of fighting and struggling with the inevitable, we can accept it and use it as a way of planning for the future.

So instead of being at the mercy of our emotions and being pulled hither and thither by our frustrations, fear, bitterness and resentment, we can begin to regain a degree of purpose and direction for our vocation. We can rediscover our spiritual composure. For we are in fact emphasizing our faith in God by putting so much hope in resurrection and our understanding that the new body may well be very different from the old.

Doing and being

One of the classic ways of coping with grief is to get busy. And one response to the lack of priestly identity today is to devise schemes and ministries that will show how much we are doing. If we can justify our vocation by saying, 'Look how much I am doing and still very few people take any notice of me,' then we can feel that we have shifted the responsibility for failure to others.

I am reminded of those intercessions you sometimes hear in services of Holy Communion when whoever is praying is so scared of the spirituality of silence that he or she feels that seemingly endless words are a substitute for a rather embarrassingly self-conscious gaze within.

An over-emphasis on what we are doing – or are meant to be doing – can disguise a spiritual pride which comes from a disinclination to depend upon God for identity and meaning.

Manufactured ministry that is church or world-centred sits uncomfortably opposite a vocation to holiness. If holiness is understood to be about difference in terms of dedication to God, we have to understand that it is not man-made. Instead it comes only as a gift from God and as the result of a determination first of all to be in his presence.

> The highly laudable aim of trying to make relevant a 2000-year-old faith – that lays great emphasis on such things as the symbolic meaning behind seed planting and sacrifice – to a world of silicon chip and cyberspace hides a blasphemy . . . For no amount of up-to-date management practice or market research and analysis will add one jot to the meaning and efficacy of covenantal love. Relevance in ministry and mission comes only when it derives its identity and purpose from the incarnate love of Christ. When this is not the case then others will rush to see only the empty tomb of our worldly dreams.[3]

I am hugely sceptical of those who want us to be a successful church and who determine this success – implicitly or explicitly – by numbers. I am not saying that this is not one way by which we measure the church and its progress but it certainly is not the only way.

Most of us at some time or other will have come across a church that is held up to be successful and full of people on

Sunday only to discover that as soon as any divergence of opinion or behaviour takes place within its membership – maybe by only one or two of its members – the congregation can exhibit the prejudice that we would normally be unsurprised to find in some communities who do not claim to live by the love of Christ.

It was Mother Teresa who said that God sent his Son not to tell us how to be successful but to show us how to love, and I rather suspect that if we lack anything it is the love of Christ deep within us.

I shall never forget attending my first clergy conference many years ago in the diocese of St Albans. At the end of his talk a local consultant psychiatrist was asked rather piously what we as ministers might do to help those who were struggling with life. The psychiatrist was not a Christian; in fact he didn't believe in God at all. In reply to the question, he paused and then looked straight at us and said, 'If you really believe in an incarnate God then why don't you make him incarnate in your lives?'

As an outsider, he alerted us to the spiritual pride that is part of inauthentic spirituality both outside and within the church. This inauthentic spirituality is based upon what we do, what we achieve, rather than who we are in relation to God. Inauthentic spirituality says that you don't have to surrender yourself to God. It emphasizes structures, techniques and programmes that begin and end with the self.

Inauthentic spirituality will understand brokenness only as failure, which is to be avoided at all costs. Inauthentic spirituality refuses to actively seek out and embrace the cross. I am constantly puzzled by the plethora of 'How To Do It' or 'How To Make It Better' books on the shelves of Christian bookshops. Very few of them, if any, actually ask what it is exactly that we are meant to believe and how exactly that impacts on our lives today. They tell us how to remodel what we have always been saying, but few have found a language that resonates the love of God with the lives of the people of the world today.

We speak of the regeneration of communities but what I want to ask is what is distinctive about the good news of Christ today that makes the difference? Why is our community to be preferred over others? What is it that makes our regeneration plans speak about God to others? And why should our presence in other communities have a transforming effect on them?

I am not talking about structures but about Spirit. If we are to pursue a calling to become a holy people, what does that mean for us as individuals? What does it demand of us? Does holiness belong to another age when people were happier to speak of the supernatural, a transcendent God and angels and all that? Does the concept of holiness itself, like so much of our faith, have to be secularized first before we can own it ourselves?

At its best this represents an earnest attempt to respond faithfully to the current crisis and climate of change. At worst it is doing Christianity without Christ just as the world can do spirituality without God. The Bible has a word for this kind of faith by which at the same time as thinking that we are holding everything together, we are at the same time holding out on God. The word is pride.

Humility: the opposite of pride

The opposite of spiritual pride is humility. But let us be sure what we mean by this. For Christian humility is often misunderstood by society as being unhelpful for at least two reasons. While our faith is Middle Eastern in its origins, it has acquired many attributes in the West normally associated with Western capitalist lifestyle.

In the West humility is seen as getting you nowhere. A humble capitalist is likely to be both poor and hungry and worst of all ignored. Christian humility – having as it does few survival attributes – is also ignored because it is seen to belong within the confines of a story that has largely been discarded. For the telling of the God story has necessarily involved the use of picture language, symbolism, mystery and myth. As a result, many come to the conclusion that it is a fairy tale that properly belongs on the shelf. It was fun to believe in when you were young but it is the sort of story you grow out of as you grow up.

Without this story, human identity becomes devoid of God and damned to a pretty hopeless existence. As a result, some go so far as to exchange an understanding of individual identity as being made in the image of God for a biological bar code. They deny there is anything unique that separates humanity from any other DNA-bearing organism. Whereas St Paul referred to Christians as temples of the Holy Spirit, there is a growing consensus that we are nothing more than elaborate machines for evolutionary survival.

To revisit our understanding of what holiness might be and how it operates within human being and becoming, we need to refresh ourselves with the unique and transforming qualities of Christian or Christ-like humility.

The word 'humble' is derived from the Latin *humilis*, meaning low, and *humus*, the ground. It is to do with being in touch with the earth. The Greek word *tapeinos* used most commonly in the New Testament documents reflects a similar kind of lowliness. This idea that human identity is delivered by being in touch with the earth is also found in Genesis where the story is told that God formed humanity from the dust of the ground into which he breathed the life of his own Spirit. The author of the second chapter of Genesis, writing in Hebrew, says that *adam* (human being as distinct from animal or plant being) was formed from *adamah* (the dust of the ground or earth, Genesis 2.7).

24

Humanity and the earth are inextricably linked. The carbon in our bodies may well have its origin in a star that was once a very long time ago somewhere out in the universe, but our humanity is formed from the earth of this planet. We are part of this creation. And our reflective awareness, reasoning and level of consciousness mean that we – of all God's creatures – can become involved in that kind of freedom of behaviour, expression and relationship in which love can make Christ incarnate. St Paul makes a contrast between human being at first and human being at last – Adam as described in Genesis and confined by the Law of Moses and Adam fulfilled in Christ who became a life-giving spirit (Romans 5.12–18; 1 Corinthians 15.45).

But while our origins and destiny are found in the earth, they are not finally defined by it. 'You are dust and to dust you shall return' (Genesis 3.19) is matched by our knowledge that in life, dust and Spirit combine and co-operate within the context of creation and re-creation. Later on, the author of the book of Ecclesiastes observes how at death 'the dust returns to the earth as it was, and the breath returns to God who gave it' (Ecclesiastes 12.7).

But we can't make ourselves humble. It isn't something that happens as a result of what you do, but rather of who you are. If we try and achieve it ourselves, we end up with some kind of manufactured piety that most people can see through immediately.

Humility and holiness go together. You cannot have one without the other. And humility – like holiness – is a gift. It happens when we begin to understand our earthiness within its divine context. For we are no ordinary dust. In us, Spirit combines with matter to produce Divine life.

While humility is a gift – rather than something we can make or earn ourselves – we pursue it as the hallmark of the Christian life. We will never know whether or not we ever attain it. Others may tell us, but if we ever consider ourselves to be holy this will be a sure sign that we are not.

When we fail to define our earthiness in these terms we cease to be grounded in God. When, however, we consider this 'God breathed dust which is me' we become both down to earth about our significance and raised up in our appreciation of the divine potential we represent.

While the secular world wants to write its own story, the Divine story gathers dust from all over the world. This dust discovers its identity in death and resurrection. It is a story that can make sense of us all.

To be called by God to be a priest, therefore, is not primarily a calling to do anything. Instead it is a vocation to be. To be humble and grounded in God. To become holy by the co-operation of the Divine Spirit with ours.

Vocation begins with an understanding of where we are and where God is in relation to us. Holiness happens when we live faithfully within this context. I would dare to suggest that this is what we lack more than anything. This humble grounded-ness. We certainly do not lack structure or programme. But perhaps we have forgotten the importance of sainthood – the calling to a holy different life – of all baptized Christians.

The Tiller report of 1983, which for some was both prophetic and seminal in the development of the ministry of the church, lists eight possible roles for the parish priest. They are: the priest as leader, pastor, a focus of community, a public spokesman, guardian of tradition, professional minister, enabler of the laity and church-builder. The report calls for increased specialization and for an end to the 'general practitioner' role and that 'in each case a job description relating to that particular post should be drawn up' as 'it is quite clear that within the ordained ministry there is a great diversity of gifts; no checklist can be compiled of those which are essential'.[4]

That is, of course, if the gifts of ordained ministry are

limited to those defined by function rather than ontology. I would argue that however we do what we attempt to do is determined by who we are, or rather who Christ is in us. Sadly, the case is being increasingly made for vocation to be determined by individuals being called because they have particular gifts or abilities suited to a function rather than a potential in prayer and the spiritual life or a more direct encounter with the God who calls.

As I say, function and ontology need not be mutually exclusive, but function without spiritual becoming is likely to produce a management that sits light to the meaning of the Divine story.

So in the working out of my vocation, who I am is more important than ever. For priestly formation – a process that continues throughout my life – has more to do with who God has called me to be, than with my reactions to the restrictions of a tradition that ties me down.

Paradoxically, it may well be that the path of holiness will at times lead me away from God. This sounds an unlikely path to humility. But this can be understood as a faithful reaction to the pressures and restrictions that I currently feel rather than a denial either of God or of my vocation.

Leaving home

Which brings us back to Jacob. It is difficult to draw out the meaning of his story as there are so many different facets to it, so let us take the main themes one at a time.

In this first chapter we are focusing upon the time when Jacob fled his home. It is customary to understand this as the result of the breakdown of his relationship with his father Isaac and brother Esau. Pushed on by his doting mother who favours him, he lies and cheats his way into apparent obscurity. Jacob as the eventual hero of the story is shown to have had a pretty Godless beginning and it is all his fault. At this stage, he is a self-centred, ambitious and deceitful person. Our sympathies lie with Isaac and Esau. It is a great story for teaching and preaching. Bad boy leaves home but eventually repents and relationships are restored. If it can happen for Jacob, it can happen for us.

It was similar for the prodigal or profligate son of whom Jesus spoke, wasn't it? Younger son rebels, leaves home, messes up, realizes what he has lost, returns and toes the line. But what about the elder son? And what about Esau? Is Esau in the story simply to show goodness and right living? Did the prodigal son and Jacob return to toe the line? I don't think so. For in both stories the return of the wayward son actually demands something of those who have stayed at home. Things don't go back to where they were. Everything is not the same again as it was before the exodus of a member of the family. When the reconciliation takes place, things have moved on. Those who have stayed where they are learn from those who have wandered off.

It is also important to consider that Jacob's journey away from the family that had nurtured him was not simply a device to reveal him as the villain so that later on we might praise him as the hero.

But if it wasn't simply because he was a self-centred and maybe evil young man, what else might have prompted Jacob to behave in the way that he did?

I want to suggest that it was because he was deeply unhappy with his traditional position in the family set-up. He was born holding on to his brother's leg not so much to symbolize that he wanted to usurp his brother's position but because he was trying to say, 'Don't forget me, I'm an individual, too. I have rights and needs for fulfilment as well.'

For the traditional way of ordering family life in his day left no room for Jacob to find fulfilment. His place in the family was defined from birth and would remain the same until his death. He was the younger brother and it was traditionally the elder brother who received both the birthright and the blessing from his father. In other words, Esau got the lot while Jacob was left with nothing.

Jacob can therefore be seen not as a self-centred, power-hungry egotist but as someone who revolted against a tradition that meant that he could find neither fulfilment nor long-term peace. The only way he could have coped with staying where he was would have been in living by a form of self-denial. To stay where he was, he would have had to decide to do whatever it took to fit in even at the expense of his own fulfilment and self-expression.

But because he was not prepared to surrender so much of himself, he was forced to move on and away from a tradition that discriminated and disempowered him and many others like him.

You might think this interpretation is a bit far-fetched. But why should we not expect the love of God to be this radical when it confronts the traditions of the world particularly when they have been incorporated into our faith in God? If by our traditions we grant false power and prosperity to a few while the majority are denied fulfilment, and if at the same time we give this abuse of tradition a god-like validity, then the demands of creative love are bound sooner or later to stand against what appears to be systematized oppression.

Jacob has a vocation and as a direct consequence is restless. He cannot find the fulfilment of that vocation within existing structures. He struggles to regain power in his own life and in so doing abuses his position. But maybe it is the only way that he and his mother feel that he has a chance to be himself. And the need to be himself – to find his own fulfilment – is what drives him on.

So having tried to get the tradition to work for him, he

finds that there is no way he can find fulfilment within it. New wine – even as early on as this – needs new wine skins. So he is forced to flee the family that has fed, clothed, loved and nurtured him to this point. He has no choice. It was either agree with the traditional way of doing things and lose himself or lose this old way of being himself and go out and find his life elsewhere.

In defence of this reading of Jacob's story, I find it interesting to note that on at least two other important occasions in his life, Jacob again shrugs off unhelpful tradition that is claustrophobic for those who long for spiritual growth.

The first is when he marries Rachel – his uncle's younger daughter – rather than Leah the elder one. According to tradition the elder daughter should marry first, but Jacob is not interested in tradition. He has fallen in love with Rachel. Love is more important than law (Genesis 29.15–30).

The second occasion is when he is dying and he asks Joseph to bring his two sons, Ephraim and Manasseh, to him so that he may bless them. Jacob's eyesight by this time is failing and Joseph puts Ephraim at Jacob's left and Manasseh at his right. However, despite Joseph's protests, old Jacob crosses his hands over and puts his right hand on the younger of the two, on Ephraim, because while Manasseh's descendants will become a great people, his younger son will be greater (Genesis 48).

As far as Jacob is concerned, never again should tradition alone dictate our future when it promotes inherited authority and power on some while denying the human and spiritual potential of others.

For very early on in his life, Jacob had come to understand that the tradition in which the majority of the members of his family found their status and lifestyle no longer promoted life.

Painful though it was and dramatic in the consequences

it would produce, Jacob realized that as far as he was concerned this tradition had died. And his greatness was in his willingness to accept this and move on. And initially, his moving on involved a moving away from God; away from the context of the blessing he had fraudulently obtained; away from the traditional family where God was worshipped and located through prayer and sacrifice.

Alien interests

However, those who have pursued a holiness of life – defined by the quality of our relationship with God that comes from a humble recognition of where we are in relation to him – have always been those who have been prepared to be rootless to a large degree.

Even those saints who have been grounded in a community or around a shrine have in themselves had a transitory aspect to their nature and faith. They invest themselves in God rather than in any human tradition or institution. They sit light to these things, which they know are only part of the passing age.

Alan Kreider reminds us that 'The word that the early Christians repeatedly adopted for themselves was a socio-legal term; *paroikoi* – "resident aliens".' These Christians believed that, because of their life in Christ, they were living in a distinctive way that had global implications. 'There was something catholic, something universal about the life that they shared with others throughout the empire and beyond; and significantly, when under pressure, they often expressed their primary identity in a simple affirmation of allegiance to Christ, "I am a Christian".'[5]

But this was more than a dislocation of these Christians from their physical environment. This was symbolic of a deeper spiritual relocation within the kingdom of God that crossed the boundary between earth and heaven. As the

31

author of the well-known *Epistle to Diognetus* from the second century reminds us:

> Christians are not different from the rest of men in nationality, speech or customs . . . They live each in his native land – but as though they were not really at home there . . . Every foreign land is for them a fatherland and every fatherland a foreign land . . . In the flesh as they are, they do not live according to the flesh. They dwell on earth, but they are citizens of heaven.[6]

With the advent of Christendom in the third and fourth centuries, some Christians confined the radical teachings of Jesus to a clerical or sectarian elite. Others defined them in such a way that they did not require them to behave in an unconventional manner in society. Now Christians were still referred to as *paroikoi* but this term no longer meant resident aliens. It now meant 'residents, parishioners, people whose distinctiveness was not that they were unlike their neighbours, but that they were unlike people in other countries whose rulers espoused some other faith'. The primary allegiance of Christians was no longer to the 'transnational family of God' but to 'people with whom they shared a common race and place'.[7]

In these early beginnings we can see how important it was for Christians to regard themselves as being essentially rootless and constantly on the move. Great harm is done to the gospel – and we deny ourselves and others of so many of God's gifts – when we try and trap the teaching of Christ within a certain structure. We often promote a kind of semi-permanence that, rather than providing spiritual security, becomes another form of physical comfort for those who would prefer to define their identity as pilgrims in a standing-still kind of way.

The pursuit of worldly permanence and a holy life are

mutually exclusive. While we are grounded in the reality of the world, our humility is such that the Spirit who enlivens this dust is one that is constantly moving over the waters of our lives to produce new life and love.

The purpose of this movement of the Spirit is the cease-less re-creation not only of humanity but also the earth on which we live and the universe we regard in awe and won-der. And those of us who are prepared to say 'yes' to this Spirit whose origin and destiny we cannot define – we know neither where he comes from nor where he goes (John 3.8) – have also to be prepared to be blown about a bit. And isn't this what we are experiencing now? Being blown about?

It is certainly not a comfortable experience. For this wind blows the cobwebs away and it asks very deep and search-ing questions concerning our tradition.

So when we think of ourselves today as aliens in a foreign land we can understand this in at least two ways: we can see it in terms of a loss of identity in a changing church, or on the other hand we can learn how best to mourn our loss of position – and identity – in a changing society and chang-ing church in order to move on. Both of these have a degree of self-pity attached to them together with a good degree of fear and insecurity. Only one of them offers any real hope for the future.

We might feel we were ordained to a certain kind of church which isn't really there any more. We might feel that where we once understood where we fitted into society and how society related to us, we discover now that most peo-ple seem to find most of their answers somewhere other than from the church.

It looks as if, in the spiritual evolution of the West at least, the majority have grown out of organized religion. For most people it is not an attractive way to find enlighten-ment. This is another death we have to face. Organized religion has a bad press. Its record in history has been marked by a great deal of intolerance and oppression. People have even used it to justify their desire or need to go to war. These incidents remain in the corporate memory longer than the great love and compassion that good faith has produced over many centuries.

So it is that we find ourselves in this difficult place where – feeling trapped by an inherited structure that should have given us freedom to be ourselves and exercise the priesthood God has given us – we long to reclaim some power over our lives.

Worn out and fed up at times, we don't want to be trapped for however many years we've got in a system that will deny us so much of what we want to claim as our destiny. So like Jacob we try and manoeuvre and manipulate the system so that we get the best out of it for ourselves. But sooner or later we have to accept that the only way out is by walking away.

Earlier on I suggested that this meant walking away from God, but what this really entails – like Jacob – is walking away from unhelpful traditions about God that lead not to further self-expression, but to a denial of opportunities.

So the life of humility may well mean that if we are to be down to earth and realistic about the current situation, we have to be prepared to regard ourselves as resident aliens. Our centre of security needs to be shifted so that instead of 'coping with the palliative care of the patient' we can become creative in the rediscovery of a cross-centred life that is placed at the heart of society.

This brings us back to our rediscovery of humility. Here we are to be earthed not primarily within the traditional institutional structures of our ancestors but through that holiness that happens wherever dust and Divine Spirit produce the possibilities of Christ in human nature.

Holiness and honesty

Whereas holiness in the Old Testament seems often to be about differentiating between sinful humanity and the God who is holy Other, in the New Testament holy separation is superseded by holy incarnation. 'The Holy has taken flesh. Holiness has now embraced what is profane (pro-fane: literally "outside the Temple").'[8]

The present ecclesiastical structures and our life within them, however, struggle to make available such a holistic approach to life. This is another reason for walking away from this god. In that we do not appear to be any different from any other human institution of overriding self-interest, we do not appeal to others. In so far as we are not grounded in the Divine life, the church occupies a life alongside society in a similar way that our life runs parallel to the life of Christ rather than the two becoming one. For holiness is not about separating ourselves from others in a 'holier than thou' kind of way.

Holiness in Christian ministry is therefore not to do with any tradition that suggests we are better than others, that we are set apart or above them, that we are exclusive or that we have anything approaching a monopoly of the Holy Spirit. When ministry becomes affected by or even attached to such ideas, these again represent a part of the tradition that we need to walk away from.

By getting real about the nature of our earthiness – in understanding humility properly – we can avoid this kind of paternalistic priestly condescension.

In the beginning God breathed life into all dust and not simply one humanly defined religious part of it. He breathed life into Jacob as well as Esau. He breathed life into those who are like us and those who are unlike us. Those from our own country and those from other countries. Those who speak and believe like us and those who do not.

Holiness consists of this faithful insight into human nature. With this in mind, we are to hold on to God in this apparently unholy mess that is me and you, us and them.

Holiness is not only about living with our lack of fulfilment as far as the world goes but also with our ungodliness. It is especially about finding God in our ungodliness.

Isn't that what Jacob did and what the prodigal son did? Isn't that what Esau and the son that stayed at home did not do – could never do – simply because they stayed where they were? (Esau only moved into a newly defined territory after he had met up again with Jacob.)

Holiness, defined in terms of being down to earth about who we are in relation to God, is a way of life that instead of denying, embraces our humanity. And everyone else's for that matter.

This life in the Spirit means that there is no part of my life – or any one else's – where I need to feel so inadequate or ashamed or sorry that I cannot come to terms with it. I am an earthy person and this is what it means to be comprised of Divine life within a worldly setting. For we can be both beautiful and beastly.

So holiness has nothing to do with respectability. Nor is it about the setting of false standards that neither those who are ordained nor those who are not can attain. Styles of Christian leadership should not be open to the interpretation that ministers are those who stand at the gates of the kingdom of God and charge an admission fee that God never requires. Instead, priests and pastors are mediators who show the world where Christ already is.

I remember vividly a trip I once made to London some time ago when I had been invited to speak about my ministry to what was a very middle-class and exclusive dining club. I should add at this point that this was before the illicit drug scene had begun to be the driving force behind so much of what is not good that goes on in inner cities – and elsewhere – today.

I duly went and delivered my talk over coffee after the meal and through a fog of cigar smoke. My jokes were clean and my talk devoid of gossip and the vote of thanks was suitably begrudging.

However, in conversation afterwards those present were quick to try and establish their credibility as church supporters or churchgoers. One even told me he was a churchwarden. I listened very carefully to what they had to say.

They believed that the Christian religion was on the whole a good thing. But I gained the impression that they found it difficult to make certain central connections about the nature of the gospel that Jesus Christ spoke about and lived. Theirs was a very privileged existence: money, security and power in abundance and a lifestyle which spoke of so great a degree of material comfort that I gained the impression that they took much for granted in a world where so many go without. (As, I am sure, would I in their position.) After a surfeit of fine food and fellowship of this kind I left.

I decided to walk back from the club where I had been wined and dined to the hotel where I was staying. It was late at night and as I walked I bought the next day's newspaper and paused to read it. As I stood and read I heard the girl's voice. It was clear and soft. There was a beauty about its tones. It sounded like the voice of an angel. She whispered gently into my ear.

I was surprised. I hadn't seen her approach. And while I didn't look directly at her I was aware of a slim, slight, pretty silhouette standing next to me. She spoke without fear, distaste or apology. She said that if I wanted, it would only cost twenty pounds. Devoid of any pretence, of any kind of formal respectability, she said that money could change hands and I could use her body for a while.

I thanked her and politely declined. She wandered off,

merging back into the shadows and I was left alone again with the morning's news. I walked on and suddenly became aware of the extraordinary contrasts of that evening. One moment I was in the smart London club speaking to its respectable members, pillars of society not to mention of their local church. Then I was in the darkness of the streets and in the company of the young woman for whom social respectability had probably gone out of the window a long time ago.

Yet what impressed me most was the honesty and dishonesty of these different people I had met.

There seemed to be a latent dishonesty about the middle-class respectability of those at dinner. There seemed to be an invisible barrier between us. They were keen to show that they had made it and that they were good at handling life. They liked to see themselves as good Christians, yet I got the impression that behind the veneer they were like most other people. Just as fallible and flawed, although of course they didn't want anyone to see this. Maybe they didn't want to accept it themselves. Above all, it seemed that there was a pretence about who they were and how they were living.

By contrast there was honesty about the girl on the street. She didn't have a voice or visage that spoke of evil. This was how she was. I don't know how she got to be like this but in that moment it didn't seem to matter. What counted was that she was being true to who she was at that time. There was no pretence here. There are those so-called respectable people who will do it for nothing with a colleague's partner after an alcoholic-fuelled dinner or office party. But this woman at least charged for it. Hers wasn't a respect conferred by society's criteria. Instead it came simply from her lack of pretence.

While the members of the black-tie dining club might probably thank God they were not like this young girl – they would probably heap entrance criteria on her if she was to enter their church – I felt that Christ would have been more at home in her company than in theirs. She had no condemnation in her heart, just a confused and probably abused experience and understanding of love.

My mind turns to the story in the Fourth Gospel where the religious leaders bring the woman caught in adultery to Jesus (John 8.1–11). They want to condemn her. They say she has forfeited her holiness and her access to God by her conduct. The men of this religion feel close to God and full of righteous indignation about all that is going on in society which contravenes their sacred tradition. To them, the woman, in her longing for love, symbolizes godlessness. As such, she is perceived to be a threat not only to the respectability of their religion but also to their relationship with God.

It seems to be a straight choice. Between our definition of holiness and his. Human religion defining conditional grace versus the unconditional divine love of our humanity that brings healing and wholeness. Human tradition versus holy embrace.

Jesus refuses to condemn the woman and tells her to go on her way. And because she is so close to Christ he was able to say to her 'Do not sin again'. By contrast, he was never able to say these words to the religious leaders, because of their unwillingness to come to terms with their earthiness together with their refusal to stand by him.

So it is not an unholy endeavour to consider walking away. It is better to walk away than to try to hijack systems that will never work for us and will never give us what we long to have.

Taking a risk to be myself

But what does it mean to walk away like this? It means that having been made to feel uncomfortable in many ways about who we are and the ministry we offer, we leave it behind. While our vocation may be one of the most important parts – or the most important part – of our life, we make the decision to free it from its institutional role. We effect its release from all the usual day-to-day parish business that we know has very little to do with our role as priests but which nevertheless occupies so much of our time.

Francis Dewar, writing in his book *Called or Collared?*, says something similar in terms of the effect of our life on the life of the Christian community. He says that what is required of the ordained person is to keep the Christian community true to what it is, to prevent it turning into a social work agency or a political party or a flower arranging network or some kind of club for preserving the status quo.[9]

This walking away, however, does not involve cutting ourselves off from God, although it may feel like this. To begin with, prayer may become harder and the presence of God increasingly difficult to detect.

Someone who recently moved from a parish to a ministry as a school chaplain told me that for the first time since his ordination he had the feeling that, free of PCCs, the care of buildings and fundraising, he had at long last the opportunity to live and work among others and pursue the vocation he felt he had once been given.

Now it is neither possible nor desirable for everyone in a parish who wants to, to resign his or her post today. But being freed from waiting by the bedside of a terminally-ill patient – if only in our minds – gives us some room to consider other options.

For a handful there will be the option of leaving stipendiary ministry and maybe becoming non-stipendiary or ministers in secular employment. Others may leave altogether. A final departure like this is certainly an attractive idea when there is no reason to think that things are going to get better in the short or even the medium term.

But this begs the question, 'What do we mean by things not getting better?' Does being better mean being better able to pay the parish share or better by the numbers we attract to church?

Does being better actually involve being different? Does it not involve moving away from where we feel we have no room to fulfil our vocation to be somewhere we are able to grow beyond the confines of ecclesiastical tradition? Doesn't it have something to do with our decision to take the initiative, being open to the life of the Spirit and being willing to be led by him into new ways of being ourselves? Maybe, then, if we can find new ways in which to be ourselves, the church will find new ways of being itself?

Life in the Spirit after all is not supposed to be predictable. While we rely upon the power and presence of God through the Holy Spirit to give us energy and vision for our lives, we may be led to wonder where God has gone. Walking away from him, as we see him at present in our community, may well mean that we have to be realistic about a certain loss of faith.

We find it difficult to locate God where we thought he was and we fail to immediately rediscover him somewhere else. So there is a journey to be made in faith where the outcome is neither clear nor assured.

If St Irenaeus was correct when he said that 'the glory of God is a human being fully alive' then this means that to a certain degree we have to take responsibility for our own identity. It is irresponsible to leave everything with God when he expects us to take responsibility for our lives.

A believing community that deprives us of our natural inheritance – that inheritance that we should all enjoy as children of God – is not a humble community in pursuit of holiness. For it denies wholeness and the integration of God and humanity, spirit and the universe, incarnation and redemption.

When, however, the gospel permits us not only to recognize our true worth but also to take responsibility for our fulfilment, we begin to relate to one another and to our surroundings in a completely different way. When this takes place, we begin to understand the sacramental nature not only of those holy things we place on altars and practices we perform in sacred places but also of everyday things in everyday life.

These are radically different priorities to those which we most often pursue. As healing goes hand in hand with wholeness, our ownership of our lives and our salvation become bound up in one another. And in the dust of our worldly hopes and ecclesiastical dreams we discover our destiny.

Here humility and holiness go hand and hand and the meek, at last inheriting the earth, are truly blessed (Matthew 5.5).

2

PRAYER IN THE NIGHT

We turn now to look at two further incidents in the life of Jacob. The first is his dream at Bethel and the second is the time when he settled down to live with the family of his uncle Laban. In the first part I want to look specifically at certain aspects of the minister's life of prayer, and in the second I want to look at the role of the priest in the community.

Meeting

So looking at the first of these two incidents, we see that Jacob has left his parents and brother and has set off for Mesopotamia. Warned by his mother to flee from his vengeful brother Esau, and told by his father to look for a wife among the daughters of his uncle Laban, he sets off into an uncertain future. He leaves Beersheba and heads towards Haran. At sunset, in a desolate place, he decides to stop for the night. Taking a stone he puts it under his head and lies down to sleep. As he sleeps, he dreams . . .

And he dreamed that there was a ladder set up on the earth, the top of it reaching to heaven; and the angels of God were ascending and descending on it. And the LORD stood beside him and said, 'I am the Lord, the God of Abraham your father and the God of Isaac; the land on which you lie I will give to you and to your offspring; and

43

your offspring shall be like the dust of the earth, and you shall spread abroad to the west and to the east and to the north and to the south; and all the families of the earth shall be blessed in you and in your offspring. Know that I am with you and will keep you wherever you go, and will bring you back to this land; for I will not leave you until I have done what I have promised you.' Then Jacob woke from his sleep and said, 'Surely the Lord is in this place – and I did not know it!' And he was afraid, and said, 'How awesome is this place! This is none other than the house of God, and this is the gate of heaven.' (Genesis 28.12–22)

Jacob has made his decision. Or, rather, having put himself in a position where there was no alternative, he turns his back on his family and the tradition that enslaved him. So Jacob has set out alone.

We can only imagine what his thoughts might have been. In his loneliness and isolation we may guess that Jacob experiences many different emotions. As he comes to terms with his loss, he expresses his grief. We may surmise therefore that he would have felt at least some degree of guilt. He had, after all, caused the break-up of his family.

Unfulfilled at home, he was unable to cope with the denial of his own vocation. He wanted to realize his potential. Living according to family traditions that made this impossible left him no alternative but to act in the way he did. He didn't really have a choice if he was going to be true to himself.

He would probably have felt not only frustrated but angry, too. Angry with his brother for not understanding. Angry with his father for not working out some compromise that could have kept them all together. Angry also at the system that meant that the elder son inherited everything of any real worth and significance.

We are not told that he weeps but we may imagine that he does as, exhausted from all that had happened and from the journey, he lies down to sleep.

As he sleeps, Jacob has this extraordinary dream about a ladder. Climbing it was not an option. Instead of promoting his own ascent, Jacob was asked to pay attention to the descent of God into his life. So it is that at the foot of the ladder he receives the promise from God that he and his descendants will be given the land on which he is lying. God also promises that Jacob's descendants will be as numerous as the specks of dust on the earth. Through them the families of the earth will be blessed.

Not bad for someone who has caused so much trouble at home. Not bad for someone who has had the courage to move away and move on. For it is unlikely that Jacob would have received this blessing had he stayed at home where God's action seemed to be confined to paternalistic blessing given at certain times to certain chosen individuals.

Instead, lying on the earth, he finds God in the night.

And it is no coincidence that the earth – the *adamah* – on which he rests becomes a symbol of all that is being promised. For here, as we saw in Chapter 1, human being – *adam* – finds its meaning from the dust of the earth that originated in the sky.

Jacob clearly has not anticipated this. For this is an awesome place: in these most unlikely conditions and in this setting heaven opens to earth. When Jacob embraces uncertainty, it is at this moment that the Creator God of the universe comes closer to him than ever before.

Jacob awakes and early in the morning dedicates the place. He gives it the name Bethel, which means 'house of God', and then he makes a vow. This vow is understood by many to be a sign of his continued arrogance. For the vow can be interpreted as Jacob's deal with God. If God will be with him, will look after him and bring him again one day to his father's house, then Jacob will pay him back.

But there is another way of understanding this vow. This is to see it not as Jacob's deal but as a statement of what Jacob expects of the God who has met him in the night.

In other words, Jacob is saying that the God who in this dream has promised him so much will surely be the God who will be with him. This God will meet his needs and, by following him, Jacob will one day find his way home again. So he makes a vow rather than a deal. He is too afraid to start making deals. His vow is that, following God's promise, the stone he sets up will mark a holy place and a tenth of all that he has he will give back to God.

There are a number of aspects to this story that can help those in ordained ministry as we reflect upon our vocation and the Divine call to be in touch both with the earth and with heaven.

Expressing our emotions

First of all, we may observe that this was a time when Jacob was probably most honest about his feelings.

This is *the second task of grief* that we come across: being true to yourself about how you feel once the reality of your loss has been faced.

While we may find it difficult to express our emotions, it is fundamental to our faith that even when feelings of grief threaten to overwhelm us, hope is not lost. Christina Rossetti reminds us:

> All in this world have been grieved,
>   Yet many have found rest.
> Our present life is as the night,
> Our future as the morning light:
> Surely the night will pass away,
> And surely will uprise the day.[1]

But when we are in the throes of grief, it can seem as if the night will never pass.

Some bereaved people cry unceasingly through this stage. They are fortunate. Others are so deeply wounded by their grief that they cannot cry at all. It can take ages before they are able to find relief from their pain.

We tend to go in and out of these emotions. Sometimes we feel as if we are coping; as if things are beginning to get better. Then something happens and we feel we are right back where we were and we feel we haven't made any progress at all.

In parish ministry, we work hard to move on in our thinking and in the development of our vocation. We seem to rediscover the energy and vision we had at the beginning only to find that there are those with agendas of their own who pull us down, hold us back. They sometimes represent the church we are trying to move away from.

Our spiritual growth can be threatened by our reactions to those who want things to remain the same as they have always been. They can make us feel guilty and disloyal because we are trying to come to terms with the fact that life is never going to be the same again.

If only those who cannot think further beyond what they have been used to in the past would leave us alone. But their questions and their faith disturb us. They make us wonder whether we have come to the right conclusion. They encourage us to kid ourselves that there really is life where we know there is death.

There are those who say that we should not express such thoughts, not give voice to our frustration. But it is right and healthy that we do. For moving on is impossible if we don't deal with the way we feel. While anger can be destructive, a misplaced understanding of Christian charity that stifles honest debate is far more damaging to our own spiritual and emotional well-being. Having recognized that we are in a kind of grieving process, we need to enter into and express the emotions of that grief.

Grief evokes feelings of powerlessness and Godlessness. We may have decided to move away from a relationship that was dying and suffocating us. But we could not have anticipated how we would feel when the realization of that death came home to us. We may feel that to some degree we have been called to leave God behind. And while we know in our minds that the God of Old and New Testaments is not really one we can be absent from, we cannot readily relocate him where we are. We are forced to come to the conclusion that while he is always with us, God often calls us to find him where we least expect.

As we search for God to become alive to us in a new way, we are forced to admit that sometimes it is in the world rather than in the church that we come across the gate of heaven. This is particularly difficult for those who have understood their vocation to spiritual leadership to be located and centred in a building. Yet it is in the world – sleeping under the stars as it were – that God can frequently be most real and intimate in his communication with us. Here we have to face up to the awful truth that it is not after all by claiming sanctity within a religion – understood by so many to exclude sinful people – that we rediscover both our roots and our future redemption. Instead it is when we move away from religion and become soiled by everyday human experience that we find that God assures us of a future, blessed beyond our dreams.

This is not to say that the church is of no use at all. It is not to suggest that our core tradition is somehow flawed. Just lost beneath hundreds of years of social and political conformity. It is highly likely that since the Christian faith began to be established and respectable some time around three hundred years following the death and resurrection of Jesus Christ, our 'churchiness' has got in the way of the gospel. One of the effects of this distortion of the gospel today can be seen when we have so little to say to a world that is growing up and taking responsibility for its life and fulfilment.

For Christ is not the reason why our society has so little time for the church. It is far more likely that the current apathy towards organized religion comes because we are seen to be more concerned with preserving good order than with promoting healing love.

In the world, our contact with God can be more immediate. In the church, unless we are very careful, human intermediaries can hinder rather than help our prayers. Liturgy can deflect us from the demands of a direct one-to-one conversation with God. But this is not to revert to some kind of pagan animism. For it was the God of Isaac and Abraham at Bethel that Jacob met and not some 'feel-good' spirit dreamt up by his own imagination or summoned by potions and magic sticks.

Where Jacob wakes up to find God in the place of stone and dust, we awake from our tears to discover that Christ is the mediator of all relatedness and relationships in the world. When our traditions hide him from the immediacy of our loves and hates, we need to walk away to find him again. Then we can learn how to live with him and allow him to reform our relationship with himself, ourselves and others.

Jacob's dream at night reminds us of Peter's dream during the day when he was told not to call profane what God had made clean (Acts 10.9–16). Together, these two dreams remind us that religion and the world, church and creation, so often unconnected, belong together. Our humility is grounded on our apprehension of Christ in all things. Whereas all creation is God-breathed, the truth behind this Spirit-generated life is revealed and mediated by Christ. Without this mediation we are likely to surrender our faith and return to some primitive form of pagan worship and lifestyle.

Holiness is supposed to be about being set apart from the world to some degree or other: 'God did not call us to impurity but in holiness' (1 Thessalonians 4.7). This is often misinterpreted to mean a withdrawal from the earth into some kind of spiritual weightlessness. Here the church is understood to be the ark where the chosen few are protected from the storms of life. But this particular boat, bobbing around on the water, not only separates those on board from the creative activity of the Spirit but in terms of social interaction is also likely eventually to leave them high and dry.

Perhaps what most sets us apart from others is our ability to locate Christ as the ground of our relationships. If this is not the case, our faith has not fulfilled its purpose and our lives will not be filled increasingly with the Divine love as they should be.

Bonhoeffer writes:

The call of Jesus teaches us that our relation to the world has been built on an illusion. All the time we thought we had enjoyed a direct relation with men and things. This is what had hindered us from faith and obedience . . . Now we learn that in the most intimate relationships of life . . . and in our duty to the community, direct relationships are impossible . . . We cannot establish direct contact outside ourselves except through him, through his word, and through our following of him. To think otherwise is to deceive ourselves.[2]

Could this be the dawn towards which we are headed? Is this the hope that we will find through our tears?

When the emotions that are related to grief reach the surface they can overpower us and reduce us to the role of spectator. Through our tears we can feel worn out and washed up. We can feel detached, and reality can take on the appearance of a dream. But when we think we are being taken over by meaninglessness and chaos, we discover that this is a dream that is divinely inspired. 'You are a chosen race, a royal priesthood, a holy nation, God's own people, in order that you may proclaim the mighty acts of him who called you out of darkness into his marvellous light' (1 Peter 2.9).

So perhaps we need to revise our understanding of the way in which the church mediates the presence of Christ. We do this by looking again at how we can be in touch with the earth while also being in the presence of God. If we were to concentrate our energies more on being in touch with the communities we seek to serve rather than in prop-ping up the institution, perhaps we would find many new ladders of descent and doorways into God.

Again, the important thing here is that we don't make it our priority to climb the ladder. There is nothing like cleri-cal ambition for killing the kingdom stone dead.

When prayer has to change

But this can be difficult if our present experience of priestly ministry is full of questions about change that affect the way in which we pray. A troubled mind like this does not make for effective, prayerful meditation.

As the principal intercessor – in the broadest sense – in a worshipping community we are likely to pray in a certain manner. However, with developments in lay and ordained ministry, the place of our particular prayers may not be as clear as it was before.

We offer the prayers of others or enable their offering to be made in formal or informal liturgy. We seek to serve the Christian community as spiritual leaders, but so much of what we assumed as our authority seems to be drifting away from us.

Moving from a 'father knows best' model to a fully collaborative one in many cases helps to empower the laity. But while the laity are feeling empowered, the clergy can feel disempowered. As a result some clergy may feel that while they are the full-time, trained professionals their role seems to be increasingly undervalued, under threat and misunderstood.

If one day in the distant future lay presidency is accepted, this will be seen by many as a further – and maybe the final – nail in the coffin. While there will be those who can accept it, others will have lost the concept of priesthood that they have grown up knowing and understanding.

When prayers are difficult in this dark place, and the spiritual life runs dry, we can drift away from spiritual leadership into management, bureaucracy and other people's initiatives. While such aspects of church life may be intrinsic to a programme of renewal, they are no substitute for that incarnate life that grounds God in everyday experience. Increased professionalism among clergy may have its benefits but if behind this there is a suggestion that this will somehow renew the spiritual life of the church and make us more humble servants, I very much doubt it will prove effective.

So much of the life of the priest centres on his or her life of prayer. It is his or her relationship with Christ that matters most. It is our 'being-with-him' or rather our constantly living in his presence[3] which forms the core of our identity and ministry. This is not to suggest that the ordained minister is the only one who is with Christ or the only one who walks with God. Nor is it to say that his or her prayers are better or more effective or more holy than those of anyone else. Nevertheless, the priest is set apart to be a person of prayer among a praying community. The effectiveness of his or her ministry depends upon this:

God normally prefers to show his wonders through those men who are more submissive to the impulse and guidance of the Holy Spirit and who, because of their intimate union with Christ and their holiness of life are able to say with St Paul, 'It is no longer I who live, but Christ who lives in me' (Galatians 2.20).[4]

So what happens when we get worn out with praying? When in the darkness and the numbness of grief we struggle to see any point in it any more?

There are those, of course, who can carry on saying the daily office throughout their ministry and into their retirement. There are others who find that in times of crisis – which can be as much about creeping apathy as it can be about sudden and searching questions – their prayers fall apart. In the darkness, God no longer seems to be around. We struggle to find him as we used to in the church. And while we recognize him in the world, we don't seem to have the words to say hello. In the honesty of our grief we wonder why it so difficult for God to answer our prayers to rebuild his church.

All these are feelings that can affect our individuality and the purpose of our lives and cause us to wonder whether by being ordained and giving so much of our lives to the church we haven't made some awful mistake.

We need to remember, however, that when we cannot pray in the way we have become accustomed to in the past, it may well be that the God of the journey is no longer where we thought he was. Or maybe he was there – is there – but having ourselves moved, we have to find him again where we are at present.

I am not suggesting that God changes his nature but that our understanding – both of ourselves and of him – develops as we grow up and as humanity grows up, too. Our pursuit of holiness is at the same time our journey into wholeness.

When this night comes, we need not assume that we have lost the power to pray. We should recognize that our feelings of guilt at our inability to pray are but a part of the grieving process. For when darkness comes upon us like this, we are quick to blame ourselves and to feel that everything is our fault. But this crisis in our prayer life is often a sign of growing maturity rather than the onset of spiritual madness. But how are we to react if all we can see in our prayers is darkness when before there was light?

Perhaps we need to learn again that holiness in a fallen world cannot be about any concept of perfection. Humility sometimes can be felt in the touch of the earth on the soles of our feet. At other times, when we trip, the collision between *adam* and *adamah* can be a painful reminder that we are not as invulnerable as we might have assumed. Light is always accompanied by darkness and love emerges through creation only slowly and painfully. There is no such thing in this world as love without pain.

God created the night along with the day and it was a part of his covenant with his people that day and night will never cease (Genesis 8.22; Jeremiah 33.20, 25). It was during the night that the Passover took place and during the night that God parted the Red Sea and later provided manna in the wilderness (Exodus 14.21). It was during the night that God spoke to individual people – not only to Jacob but also to Balaam, Gideon, Nathan, Solomon and others.[5]

So we are oversimplifying matters when we confine the presence of God to the prayer of the day and assume his absence during the prayer of the night.

St Ignatius in his Exercises – and elsewhere in his letters – speaks of the need to handle carefully both our times of consolation and desolation if we are to enter into a deeper relationship with God. Times of true consolation are a gift from God and we are filled with a love for God and through him for creation. But these are to be carefully handled for a number of reasons. Not the least of these is in case in our renewed love we get carried away and make decisions and judgements which belong not to God but to our own plans.[6] This consolation is not with us all the time but is given for our profit according to God's plan for our lives.

Times of desolation are times when, in an absence of consolation, we are plunged into sadness and it is difficult to pray with any devotion. Our enthusiasm dwindles and we feel that everything we have done counts for nothing.[7] Again, God himself can be the origin of these feelings but they can also come from a negative source that seeks our destruction. Ignatius counsels that in times of desolation we should make no changes and stand firm and constant in the resolutions and decisions that were made before the onset of desolation. For when we are down like this we are open to being led astray from our vocation.[8]

But it doesn't feel that we have that luxury. Sometimes decisions have to be made in darkness, but when they do, how should we pray?

First we need to ask ourselves whether this night has come because we have been lazy or unfocused. If so, as Ignatius and many others suggest, we should redouble our efforts to erect the structures of prayer which we have always sought to follow and which form the basis of our ministry. But if, on the other hand, the darkness has come at God's behest, our prime concern should be to make sure we are open to God who is within it.

God was able to speak to Jacob in the night because Jacob had remained in touch with his earthiness, with his true identity. He sleeps on the ground. Dust among dust. He is neither distant nor proud. He does not initiate this meeting. He is in a new and unfamiliar place. He is devoid of any spiritual aids or guides. All he can do is to keep in touch.

Keeping in touch like this is to know that our relationship with God does not start when we pray and stop when we cease to pray, any more than we cease to live when we hold our breath, or that our love stops when we are separated from our partners.

As one of our Eucharistic Prayers proclaims:

How wonderful the work of your hands, O Lord.
As a mother tenderly gathers her children,
you embraced a people as your own.
When they turned away and rebelled
your love remained steadfast.
From them you raised up Jesus our Saviour, born of
    Mary,
to be the living bread,
in whom all our hungers are satisfied.[9]

The constancy of the love of God is matched in our own experience by what Simone Weil refers to as the 'implicit love of God'.[10]

This consists of experiences in which God is present though unrealised by the person involved in the experience. These experiences are those that are constituted by the apprehension of the beauty of the world, the love of our neighbour, and the simple participation in the religious acts of the worshipping Church.

It is all the more important, therefore, in the prayer of the night – when God seems distant and our words won't work – that we avoid anything and everything that prevents us from simply being grounded in the reality which is God. Jacob will have questioned his own conduct and the existence of God. He may have considered taking a different route, away from Laban and any reminder of a family that had hurt him so much. But he didn't. And as a result he remained in touch with the earth and therefore with heaven.

We need also – Ignatius seems to be saying – to preserve our desolation and keep it pure. It is a time when demonic powers can drag us away, tempting us by the affairs of the world.

We should not be surprised, therefore, when formal prayer and traditional patterns of prayer may fail to satisfy us during this time. So we look to pray in whatever way we can.

The problem of the functional analysis of the spiritual life comes to the forefront here as it suggests that we can't 'be' priests if we don't 'do' praying. This is, of course, nonsense. For when darkness descends, our praying is centred more than ever upon our being and not our doing. So when the guilt, fear, anger and bitterness subside and we find those times of peace that come between the peaks and troughs of emotion, we may have the confidence to reach out in prayer and hope by simply being ourselves. Nothing more. Nothing less.

One of the greatest comforts we can have in this life is the unconditional love of another. Simply knowing that we are loved for being who we are provides meaning and orientation for both soul and body. If we are fortunate to experience this through our human relationships, how much more true must it be of our relationship with God?

So as we learn to live with our uncertainties, we are able to avoid the desire to make things up as we go along or to give a fraudulent exposition of the gospel we no longer believe in. We live instead where the life of the priest should most commonly be found, at the intersection between death and resurrection, where faith meets doubt head on and light overcomes darkness.

So through both the times of spiritual fullness and emptiness we are to remain with God. His presence or absence does not depend upon our emotional awareness but on our spiritual location. Prayer offered from this point of view is never pointless.

We can only be where we believe God wants us to be. This may for now be a lonely and desolate and frightening place. A place where we are more likely than ever to express our emotions, our anger, frustration and heartbreak at broken promises and shattered dreams.

It may well be that here our weakness is our strength and our grief is a prelude to our joy.

So what might this say to our present experience of changing world and changing church? I think we are right to proclaim that God is not absent but very much with us along this journey. Rather than being left behind by change, God is actually behind it and us. And we have no alternative but to live by a hope that this journey – which is not one we would necessarily have chosen for ourselves – will eventually take us home again.

Meaning and mercy in community

It is time now to remind ourselves of the way in which Jacob arrives at his uncle's household, how he marries Rachel and Leah, and how one daughter, Dinah, is born along with the sons whose descendants will make up the people of Israel.

By common sense, diplomacy, tact and guile, Jacob establishes himself and builds up not only his family but also his wealth. Once again, we see how ill at ease he is with tradition. He wants to marry Rachel because he has fallen in love with her. Tradition demanded that he married Leah first. But he clearly believes that the fulfilment of love takes precedence over the demands of the law despite Laban's attempt to abide by the customs of his country. So it is that Jacob ends up marrying both sisters, but it was Rachel he married first and favoured later, at least through her son Joseph (Genesis 29 and 30).

Jacob seems to have borne the traits of a good business-man. As time passes, his flocks increase in number and strength while the flocks of Laban apparently decline. But Laban is not above exploiting the presence of Jacob and continues to try and take advantage of him. Eventually the God of Bethel speaks to Jacob once more and tells him to prepare to make his journey home, to the land where he was born.

So Jacob leaves, yet he feels hard done by and loses his temper when Laban pursues him, furious about his sudden departure and the loss of his household gods.

Jacob says to Laban:

These twenty years I have been with you; your ewes and your female goats have not miscarried, and I have not eaten the rams of your flocks. That which was torn by wild beasts I did not bring to you; I bore the loss of it my-self; of my hand you required it, whether stolen by day or stolen by night. It was like this with me: by day the heat consumed me, and the cold by night, and my sleep fled from my eyes. These twenty years I have been in your house; I served you for fourteen years for your two daughters, and six years for your flock, and you have changed my wages ten times. If the God of my father, the God of Abraham and the Fear of Isaac, had not been on my side, surely now you would have sent me away empty-handed. God saw my affliction and the labour of my hands, and rebuked you last night. (Genesis 31.38–42)

This sounds a bit like an incumbent who has just told his PCC that he is leaving the parish after eight years when everyone had taken it for granted that he would stay until he retired. The parishioners cannot contemplate why anyone would want to move away from them. They have forgotten to test their own comfortable assumptions against the reality of the stresses of his day-to-day life.

Parish priests are of course by the very nature of the licence that the bishop gives them both grounded in a geographical area, a parish, and also within a community, the people who live in that area.

Here it is an enormous privilege to be given the direct access that parish ministry can provide into the lives of others who are often strangers. We share the joys and sorrows of others. At times we find this energizing and at other times completely draining. The cost of our discipleship can be considerable and often affects our loved ones and families as well.

When times are bad, like Jacob, we long to hear the call from God to move on. When vision and energy are lacking, it is tempting to move to an 'easier' parish which happens to be adjacent to an excellent golf course – at a time when we wish to improve our handicap – or to a church which is situated next to a marina – where we can purchase a boat and sail to our heart's content.

Yet more often than not the answer to our prayers is along the lines of, 'This is where I put you and this is where I want you to stay. For it is here that I want you to work out your salvation alongside the salvation of those who have been entrusted to your care.' This is a difficult answer to hear and even harder to live by. Yet isn't our vocation about taking up our cross – rather than our golf clubs, sailing kit or business portfolio – and following Christ?

At a time when 'obedience' is unfashionable, I have come to the conclusion over the years that our ordained ministry would be much stronger and more effective if we listened more closely to the Spirit of God in terms of deciding where we should go, how long we should stay and when we should move on. This might mean we have just one or two or ten different ministries but in the end whatever we will have done will have been accomplished out of obedience to God.

I realize this is a hard thing to say but so often we can move and minister around the place motivated by reasons such as housing, local amenities and what we feel we might have to give to a new parish. But some of the most powerful ministries in parishes have been exercised by those whose curriculum vitae hasn't immediately matched up with the parish profile. When interviewed, such people could not display any particular gifts that were relevant to the statement of needs of the parish. Nevertheless it was agreed that God had called them to that place and their ministry flourished.

When patrons, PCCs and bishops have made such appointments, they have often found that the new incumbent discovers or develops the most appropriate yet unexpected gifts to guide that particular Christian community into its next stage of development.

So in the parish we cannot divorce ourselves from those whom God has called us to be with. Archbishop Michael Ramsey, addressing those who were on their pre-ordination retreat, talks about the parish priest as a person of prayer by saying, 'We are called, near to Jesus and with Jesus and in Jesus, *to be with God with the people on our heart.*' This is in fact what we promise we will do when we agree to be diligent in prayer. 'You will be promising to be daily with God with the people on your heart.'[11] Ramsey goes on to say that often 'transcendence is to be found in the midst of secular experience and not apart from it'.[12]

This begs all sorts of questions to do with meaning. We have been discussing Jacob's meeting with God in prayer and now we are looking at the meaning this gave to his life. This, in turn, makes us consider how the way we meet with

God in prayer affects the way that we are with other people in the community.

Archbishop Rowan Williams writes, 'How you represent God affects what you are going to find possible for yourself and for the human community.'[13] So meeting and meaning are bound together by the way in which the ground of our being in God gives us a basis for our meetings with others.

If our representation of God in the community is wholly Other – transcendence without immanence – then we are likely to find ourselves several feet above the ground most other mortals tread; more at home in the church building than in the supermarket or shopping mall. As a consequence, the community will feel that God is largely disconnected from everyday life and a figure of respect and sometimes fear or even ridicule rather than love.

The model of ministry delivered in terms of eliciting respect and sometimes fear has its attractions. Discipleship levied on others by the 'imperial decree' of the incumbent is likely to be far less draining than that other model that involves openness, companionship and healing. The former calls for little self-giving while the latter calls for that kind of creative love where both priest and people share vulnerability, and by mutual respect agree to grow together.

There are many other models of ministry that we can describe – I have simply given two that are diametrically opposed to one other – but whatever model we prefer, or decide to make our own, will nevertheless be based upon 'being daily with God with the people on your heart'.

Jacob first headed off towards the land of the East because he was afraid of losing his life. This was not simply due to the threats of his brother Esau. It was because he found that in order to be himself he had to walk away from a tradition that reduced him to a second-class kind of existence and denied him his identity.

Jacob became a member of the family of Laban because he fell in love. But in the working out of that love he was forced to do a number of things, and it is to these that we now turn.

First, he had to hold on to the love he had found. He nourished it and cared for it and did all he could to preserve it. It was Rachel whom he loved and despite being surrounded by the demands – and no doubt some delights of other companions – it was to her that he was most committed and remained covenanted even when she failed to conceive.

It is highly significant that it was from this loving relationship – rather than the ones demanded by tradition – that Joseph was born. And Joseph would play a crucial part in the next stage of the development of the people of Israel. In due course Joseph, too, like his father and his grandfather, would enter into this same cycle of leaving home, meeting God and finding meaning in a new community and moving on from there to a place of reintegration. The kind of church we will become in the future may well be largely determined by our ability to hold on to the love of Christ at the centre of our life and service.

Second, Jacob had to realize that the tradition he was so keen to get away from also existed in the new community he had joined and where presumably he had hoped life and relationships would be different. So having married Rachel, he also married Leah as a compromise to get what he wanted. In the end the compromise worked well and from it came the twelve tribes of Israel. We would do well to remember that not all compromise is a sign of weakness. Unbending fundamentalism of any kind can cheat us of opportunities for growth by which – while holding on to the love of Christ – we find ways of reconnecting with those we depend on to some degree or other and without whom we would not even exist.

If Jacob had refused to compromise, the history of the Israelites would have been dramatically different. Jacob realized that while achieving his own freedom, he also had to work within the existing structures, imperfect though they were. But he not only worked with them, he embraced them in such a way that they became the source of new life for both himself and his immediate family.

Third, Jacob had to learn how to look after himself. His mother Rebekah by all accounts had spoilt him. But here among Laban's family he had to earn his keep. No one was going to give him a free ride or house and feed him for nothing. Sometimes we are reluctant to stand on our own two feet because for so long we have been used to being propped up by others. While the stipendiary minister is not paid for what he or she does, some of the comforts that come with parish life can make us at times rather complacent.

So Jacob immersed himself in the life of the community and therefore in the life of ordinary people. He worked as they did, he shared with them the heat of the sun by day and the cold of the night. He knew times of profit and dearth, times when others helped and gave and times when they turned their backs and stole what he had from him.

So we can see that while Jacob was not a priest licensed to a locality and a community, his spiritual journey – which moved from loss to meeting and now meaning – matches ours in many ways.

I suppose Jacob could have stayed at Bethel instead of moving on to be with Laban. He could have remained by his holy shrine and waited for other people to come to him. He could have justified this by preserving the sanctity of Bethel and preaching and ministering on occasions as life brought him into contact with others as their journeys brought them his way. But if he had done this, he would not have fulfilled the Divine purpose for his life. Although when he was at Bethel he must have wondered what on earth lay ahead of him.

This is not to suggest that there are not those special 'thin' places where holy shrines and places of prayer have been established where that which separates heaven and earth is all but gone. While there are many abroad, most of us have our own special places within the British Isles such as Lindisfarne, Iona and Walsingham. My favourite place is the shrine of St Melangell in North Wales where some have heard angels singing in a church rebuilt by much faith and prayer.[14]

These are places where many discover or rediscover their faith and encounter the healing presence of God. Sometimes I think these places, 'given' to us by the obedient and prayerful lives of saints in the past, will become the focus for the re-evangelism of our society, that is, if we learn how to make the most of them.

In addition to these places of pilgrimage, however, there is that mission that takes place as an inevitable consequence of the lives of those whose minds are centred on Christ and whose hearts are full of divine love. These 'living human shrines' take the gospel to those places and people whose divine potential has so far been desecrated by agendas of survival, power and the longing for physical permanence and perfection.

We are told that there is much interest in spirituality today, yet people by and large fail to find this in the church. This may be because both clergy and laity have not looked hard enough at the way we represent God in ourselves. The holiness of our shrines is not matched by the holiness of our lives.

So we come to *the third task of grief.* So far we have looked at accepting loss as a reality and entering the emotions of grief. The third task of grief is about acquiring new skills.

Hitherto we have been dealing with aspects of the dying process. Now we begin to look at the ways in which we can discover new opportunities for personal growth. So we turn now from death to the processes of resurrection.

Later on we will be looking at our reintegration into the tradition. But for now we concentrate on thinking about the nature of our vocation in terms of how we might understand our life as priests in the community.

I have suggested that in the current climate there is a need to move away from that tradition in the church which denies us self-expression in our ministry and which also prevents us from being the people of God that we are called to be.

It is important that as we turn our backs on these restricting aspects of church life – and it is up to each individual to decide which aspects of their vocations and tradition collide – that we do not regard this as turning our backs on God. We should instead view such developments as the legitimate pursuit of our service of Christ. Provided we do not deny the processes of love nor turn our backs on the guidance of the Holy Spirit, we can operate with a clear conscience in this regard. So in making changes in our ministry and thereby provoking debate and change in our local Christian communities, we can assure others that we are not denying Christ or our vocation. On the contrary, we are learning the way to rediscover God – and our faith – in the night.

So how might we be in the community in such a way that we can hold on to the insights we have gained? For we must be very careful not to surrender these insights to the many pressures of parish life which will probably not have changed while we have been away.

When going through the grieving process – while we are acquiring new skills – we naturally hold on even tighter to those who are close to us and mean the most. This may be a spouse, partner or friend.

When the object of our love – in this case the church of unhelpful and inhibiting tradition – has died and finally we find that we are ready to move on – and the time all this takes is different for all of us – we begin to feel that we dare to reinvest in relationships. Those that are good and give us energy, those where we can be ourselves and find meaning, become all the more precious. Now we devote a great deal of time and devotion to making sure that we do them justice. In doing this we acquire the skill of being life-minded rather than death-minded.

This gives us the courage and purpose to acquire new skills in our contact with a wider circle of people. To begin with, we take pride in accomplishing small and seemingly insignificant tasks with them. While we are not the same as we were before we had to face this death, others around us are very much the same. But the way we relate to them is likely to be different. So we learn to reconnect, to overcome places that hold feelings and memories of death for us. We learn to say 'yes' once again and we are prepared to ask for help. Most important of all, healthy, balanced progress at this stage happens when we are prepared to work with others from our own weaknesses rather than from our strengths.

So we adopt a different kind of incarnational loving. For we are now able – because of what we have been through – to work with others in a spirit of collaboration and even compromise so that the Spirit that flows through us may also flow through others.

Instead of calling people to where we are – or calling people to change the system straightaway to a new way of doing things – like Jacob we re-engage with what is already there. But we do this in a new way: both daily with God and with the people on our hearts.

As we do this, we are reminded again of representing God to others in such a way that we can be authentic to ourselves. For we have become so grounded within ourselves that we are free to live with, accept and do justice to, the various aspects of ourselves without being denied any of this by a system that does not suit us.

So there is room within my self for me to love myself as God has called me to. Moreover, my faith by its very nature enhances rather than inhibits my personal development. All this means that while I may feel something of an identity crisis in terms of my ministry today within the church, I need not lose sight of the intrinsic worth of my vocation.

In fact, I can affirm it and hold on to it. And I should nurture it and cherish it. At the same time, I should not become depressed when this desire for humility and holiness is challenged by my innate fallenness.

Aware of our weaknesses and working on them to deny increasingly the power they have over us and the way they can affect us, we need not feel that we are therefore excluded from the life of the saints, the holy ones of God. For sanctity, as we have seen, is frequently found and formed from the unlikely material of our failed attempts to be good pastors and priests, and even good people.

For we are not after all about the pursuit of goodness. Holiness is about the pursuit of Godliness and there is a big difference between this and any desire for goodness.

I have no illusions any more about trying to be good. I just hope to be grounded in God and in the reality of his creation. I aim to bring God to bear on myself in such a way that wherever I am, there is constant and ceaseless prayer going on which is about the interaction between Holy Spirit and this matter of me to which I referred earlier.

If we disengage with our traditional frustrations and re-engage later, freer and stronger, our excitement at this resurrection should not be denied by a realization that despite this spiritual progress we are still – for the time being at least – the same old sinful selves we ever were.

It is here that we earn our living, not by any inherited piety, nor by any kind of holiness we feel we might have received in some kind of apostolic succession of saintliness. Here we are who we are by the co-operation of human spirit with Divine Holy Spirit.

The fruits of our labours, which are in the flocks that are built up around us – which, again like Jacob, some will feed and others will steal – are based upon this ministry in and alongside the world.

While we do this, we learn about the humility that comes about in our being alongside others and in our acknowledgement of what we have in common rather than in focusing on what keeps us apart.

Christ is found within the lives of others. His is not a divinity that is injected by ecclesiastical syringe from some place above where most people live. The parish priest earns his or her keep as life is celebrated in its sharing, rather than by being paid for the spiritual wisdom that he or she might scatter from the pulpit or chancel step on Sundays.

As part of our vocation we look first within ourselves for that truth that Jesus says can set us free. Having done this, we are called to look for it in others – rather than impose it on them – so that we can identify and celebrate our freedom together. And when we come across those who have yet to discover the truth, we simply share that love that can set them free as well.

So far I have suggested that by understanding the meaning of humility we are able to transform our relationships with others. We can do this because humility generates a realistic understanding of how human nature can co-operate and combine with Divine nature. Yet humility also transforms our relationships with those whom we seek to serve because truth is not some abstract principle to be admired and manipulated by clever words and concepts. For truth is to be found most of all in the struggle of love over fear, of life over death, that is the basis of all our lives. Truth is to be discovered in this magnificent mess of human becoming which is me.

For the truth of humanity is that we are made in the image of God. Whereas pride obscures this from our minds, humility reveals it. And we respond to it in others by showing mercy to them.

This invitation to be merciful challenges straightaway so much of the way we relate to one another and to the other members of our worshipping community. Without mercy, all hopes of pursuing vocational holiness will be thwarted.

We could probably quickly and easily condemn ourselves for showing very little mercy in our relationships. Without true humility, mercy is reduced to fake interest in the fortunes and misfortunes of others, to listening to the stories of others while our minds are elsewhere. Most of us know how insignificant you can be made to feel when the person you are speaking to is not looking back at you but over your shoulder towards someone else he or she would much rather be talking to. When we are guilty of this it is often because we are suffering from a kind of compassion fatigue. This creeps up on us when our caring is too costly because it comes purely from ourselves rather than from the Christ who lives in us.

St Bernard of Clairvaux in addressing his monks about holiness says that this is the reason why in the Sermon on the Mount Christ spoke of those who show mercy before he spoke of those that are pure in heart. For those who show mercy get to find the truth about others when they show mercy to them. This mercy that comes from humility helps us to have sympathy for others and joins us together in Christian charity. As Bernard says:

For the merciful rejoice at the fortunes of their neighbours, and are sad for their misfortunes, just as if they were their

own. And if anyone is weak, they feel his weakness; if anyone falls, they long to help him up ... this love of their
brethren so cleanses their hearts and strengthens their re-
solve that they find great delight in contemplating the truth
in their own nature ... But if a man does not join himself
in love of his fellow men, but instead laughs at those that
weep and belittles the joys of the happy, he cannot possi-
bly discover the truth in those around him because he has
no feeling for them.[15]

Having eyes of mercy means also that we recognize in
others the truth of what or who they – rather than we – love
the most. We regard them not according to our plans or our
likes and dislikes but theirs. We learn to see also where and
how they – like us – compromise with tradition. Rather
than condemning it as a weakness to be despised, we now
understand this compromise as a natural part of what it
takes to live within the creative tension of what we would
like to be, within an environment which allows us only a
fraction of the freedom we need to achieve this.

Now we try and understand what it takes for others to
earn their keep in a different way from us. This is likely to
lead us to celebrate the faith that others already have rather
than bemoan the faith they do not have.

When hard pressed, we can remain in grief and negativity.
However, by working our way through the tasks of grief –
and they come in any order and we can revisit them any
number of times until we have worked through them – we
can become positive in the face of adversity. We can even
find the strength to affirm others who may be causing us
pain or frustration for any number of reasons.

When he was confronted by Laban in the hill-country of
Gilead, Jacob's sense of injustice came not from a desire for
self-justification or the desire to return like with like.
Instead it came from a deep-seated pain, which makes itself

known in an attitude that says, 'Look, I tried so hard to live a godly life among you that I developed a merciful attitude to you and yet you accuse me of cheating you.'

Our anger, fear and frustration therefore frequently arise from our pursuit of that kind of humility without which holiness is not possible. This humility produces a special way for us to be in community and communion with others.

As we learn to find divinity in our own weaknesses and fears, we learn to recognize it in others. By so contemplating the God who lives in and through the struggling humanity and divinity of others, we learn to gaze upon God. Give me this gaze any day rather than the graphs drawn by others by which they think they can predict either my supposed success or failure. For my gazing upon God sets me free to serve him away from worldly criteria of success.

St Bernard says that this relationship in community and communion with others is a Christ-like way of being human. It affirms both the humanity and divinity of others. For, 'the mercy he brought was not that which he had from all eternity in the bliss of His divinity, but the mercy he had discovered in His human nature through the lowly estate in to which he had put Himself. So it was the mercy that He learned on earth that completed the labour of love begun by the mercy of the eternal God.'[16]

Church community, of course, is constantly changing. There are those changes to which I have alluded which come about as a direct result of financial constraints. There is increased pastoral reorganization and greater pressure on stipendiary priests to take on more responsibility, often by taking on the care and oversight of additional parishes and parts of other parishes.

There are other changes that are happening to church community as well. These arise from a commitment to react positively to the financial crisis by becoming proactive in determining a new shape of church for the future. They can also come about because there is a strong desire to 'be church' in a different way from before, so as to ground the life of the church in the life of the community.

Whatever the reason for these changes, they will be short term and of limited effect if they are not first and foremost changes in community that are based upon changes in our understanding of the identity of that community and the individuals within it.

It is no good 'being church' in a different way structurally – as house church, liquid church, cell church and so on – if we are going to continue to live a gospel that is based upon a fundamental confusion between the meaning of goodness and Godliness. Like Jacob, we cannot turn our backs on the developing nature of tradition. Nor can we deny the work of the Holy Spirit as he continues to bring an ever-increasing understanding of what it means to be in communion with Christ.

We can, however, take seriously the call for mercy: 'Blessed are the merciful, for they will receive mercy' (Matthew 5.7).

3

WALKING WOUNDED

Wrestling with reintegration

Over the last two chapters we have been on a journey with Jacob. We have left home, met with God in the night and looked at ways of finding meaning in community.

Along the road we have looked at the nature of Christian humility. We have understood holiness to consist of faithful Godliness within daily living. We have unearthed the fruit of this spiritual endeavour and understood it to be about how we have mercy first on ourselves and then on others. We have also recognized the need to work through the tasks of grief, understanding our loss, expressing our emotions and acquiring new skills. At the same time we have worked our way through death to resurrection.

In this final chapter I want to look at another aspect of our journey into resurrection. To help us do this I want to revisit what we refer to as the story of Jacob's wrestling match at Peniel. I want to try and understand this in the context of Jacob's eventual reconciliation with his brother Esau and his return to live – at least initially in Shechem – in the land of Canaan.

I want to look now at how we might put what we have learned along this way into practice. I want to consider what the practical implications of this journey will be. How should we be with others when we return to make friends with them again and set up our homes among them?

I have called this 'wrestling with reintegration' because no matter how we might think of setting about the task of vocational holiness afresh, the doing of it will be much harder than the thinking about it. We should not underestimate the challenge. For it will require all our strength and commitment to put even the smallest change into practice.

It is, of course, extremely important that our quest for humility does not bite the dust in face of opposition. The final task of grief therefore is the process whereby we reinvest our energy in new ways.

So this is not about how we should think about approaching our vocation in terms of humility and holiness but about how we should live it.

So we return to Jacob's story:

Jacob was left alone; and a man wrestled with him until daybreak. When the man saw that he did not prevail against Jacob, he struck him on the hip socket; and Jacob's hip was put out of joint as he wrestled with him. Then he said, 'Let me go, for the day is breaking.' But Jacob said, 'I will not let you go, unless you bless me.' So he said to him, 'What is your name?' And he said, 'Jacob.' Then the man said, 'You shall no longer be called Jacob, but Israel, for you have striven with God and with humans, and have prevailed.' Then Jacob asked him, 'Please tell me your name.' But he said, 'Why is it that you ask my name?' And there he blessed him. So Jacob called the place Peniel, saying, 'For I have seen God face to face, and yet my life is preserved.' The sun rose upon him as he passed Peniel, limping because of his hip. (Genesis 32.24–31)

The background to this story is fear. Jacob in obedience to his vocation is returning to the land of Esau. Here he plans to make friends again with his brother. But he is afraid that this reconciliation will fail. Jacob is fearful of his brother's continued anger and resentment because of the way he had cheated and betrayed him in the past.

Jacob sends messengers and his animals and servants ahead of him in two groups. Then he also sends his own family across the river Jabbok while he waits behind. His fears have grown since he heard that Esau is already on his way to meet him, bringing four hundred men who clearly outnumbered those with him. Once again he is alone in the night.

Fear of becoming lost again

We have been talking about making sense of vocational holiness in the present climate. So much is changing and we can sense the significance of our ministry diminishing in the eyes of many. We lack the identity we once had and feel under threat. But it is not only here that we feel forced into a system that frightens us with a loss of identity and even a loss of life.

For it would be true to say that vocation always involves this kind of fear. And if it doesn't, it is because we do not truly understand what we are up against both in the world and especially within the church.

When we engage with the world, we are far less likely to be hurt deeply than when we are working with our fellow members of the church. This doesn't seem to make sense. We can't help thinking it shouldn't be like this. It ought to be the other way around. We should be supported by the love of the church to go out and minister to the world. Maybe it is because we ask more of our fellow Christians than we do of others. Maybe we are more open and there-fore more vulnerable to them. Maybe there are other – less comfortable – reasons as well.

Sadly it is often those who don't 'go to church' who end

up binding up the wounds our fellow Christians have inflicted on us. Sometimes, even, it takes them to restore our faith in humanity.

The story of Jacob is about someone who struggles to find his identity. Inherited tradition that was divorced from the processes of balanced human becoming denied him his desire to experience 'life in all its fullness'.

So he went away to try and become the person he wanted to be. He left home and loved ones to discover his destiny. He had to do this if he was to survive. And to a large extent it worked for him. Because he lost himself, he found himself. (This is the kind of paradoxical behaviour that is encouraged much later in the Gospels: for example Matthew 10.39.)

But – and this is the difficult part – Jacob could only complete this journey by returning in the end to the place and the people who had been the cause of his distress in the beginning. Few of us, I suspect, have been called to turn our backs on the pain of creation and seek a safe pleasure zone where we will not be threatened or mistreated again.

Redemption does not happen when we run away. Nor does it take place when we rush to the rescue of others. Running away isolates us from the community we are supposed to serve. Rescuing others denies them their power to move on when the time is right.

As we move away from models of ministry based upon 'justification by doing' we move towards more helpful models of 'sanctification by being'. For redemption comes about when we remain with and alongside the pain that threatens us and others. But because we have made the journey, we handle the pain in a different way from before. This time, instead of being subject to a pain that stifles and cripples us, we use it in a creative way that brings fresh insight and new ways of behaviour.

Jesus reminds us later on that even a devout faith in God

becomes fraudulent if it does not involve us in at least attempting a reconciliation with our enemies. In order to move on, we have to learn how to make friends with those who oppress us, those who have caused us pain in the past. We cannot present our gifts on the altar unless we have first worked to achieve harmony in our everyday lives (Matthew 5.23). This may involve a remaking of actual relationships. Or when this is not possible, we learn how to find a reconciliation in our heart that frees us from repetitive and unhealthy feelings and responses.

This, of course, is far from straightforward, particularly if we do not see the spirit of reconciliation in others. There may be times when we think that 'this holy dust that is me' is living close to God, and 'the holy dust that is other people' has been disfigured by what we rightly or wrongly perceive as their absence from God. Why should we go back to them?

While on occasion we may find healing for ourselves outside the traditional system, the harsh truth is that if God still calls us to serve him in and through the church, our healing has to achieve some balanced relationship with those who persecute us. To some degree or other this must have been true for clergy and their counterparts of every generation as they have at times struggled with the dynamics of human relationships within the church.

Within a parish it is natural at times to seek refuge in the parsonage house. Here what is meant to be our home can resemble a fortress. When we feel trapped by unreasonable expectations of pushy parishioners, or when someone has said or done something that has hurt us very deeply, we retreat behind these walls. And when we are in pain we can fire missiles at others from the battlements of the vicarage and plot how best to get our own back. We react to our pain by extracting revenge. But – unless we have lost all hope – we know that this will not do.

Fear and love

The gospel reveals that if healing is to take place, fear has to be overcome by love. And – worse still – the church is supposed to model this kind of healing community to the world.

The world is meant to look at our relationships with envy. The manner in which we get on with one another is supposed to make the world want to know about the God who gives us such understanding of one another. Seeing our love for one another, others are meant to want to learn how to love like this, too. It was this deep sacrificial love of the early Christian communities that had such a strong impact on others. The pagan world could not at times believe the selfless love and devotion they saw.

So we should not be surprised when God tells Jacob to make his way back home. It was the only way Jacob could go and finally be true to himself and to his calling. But he could not of course go back and be the person he was before. He had to hold on tight to his new identity.

To return simply and be a doormat for others, and fit in where he had once been, would have been a denial of all that God had helped him to grow into. So perhaps Jacob was afraid of this as well. Not simply that Esau might take away his life by killing him but that in being back with Esau he might lose his identity again.

So our regular reinvention and reintegration is an intrinsic part of the Christian life. But it is not restricted to those times of great retreat such as I have been describing when we make life-changing or ministry-changing decisions. Reinvention and reintegration are also a part of our daily lives.

If we do not try to deal with the causes of our unease, we are more than likely to make the same mistake again. And as we desire not to sin in this way again we become a little more like the person God has called us to be.

So as we become increasingly involved in the life of God, the Spirit helps us to reinvent ourselves in a Christ-like way, or, as St Paul puts it, we are 'transformed from one degree of glory to another' (2 Corinthians 3.18). And, of course, while we can all make numerous decisions about how we are going to do things differently – how we are going to be different with others – we cannot do this privately, alone in a room. We have to go and work out these resolutions among our families and loved ones, our worshipping communities and in society.

Both of these aspects of our personal development – our reinvention and reintegration – are needed in the pursuit of a humble and holy life. We co-operate with God not only in our inner spiritual life but also – and at the same time – in the living out of that divine conversation between our spirit and that of others.

We can be afraid of trying this. For any attempt to pursue the way of creative love has no assured outcome. We have no way of knowing whether, simply because we have grown up and are committed to sharing this new way of being ourselves with others, they will either understand or accept us.

When talking about transforming priesthood, Robin Greenwood reminds us that loving relationships consist of maintaining a balance between the needs and expectations of different parties. He says:

Nothing can be worthy of the name 'salvation', 'liberation', or 'freedom' . . . that represents freedom for some, at the expense of, or through the exclusion of, others . . . To be subject to one's own destiny . . . is deliberately to mirror the image of God by being externally orientated in creativity and reconciliation and choosing to align one's intentions with those of God. Dialogue here means that, on God's side at least, there is respect for freedom and independence and an absence of overdetermination.[1]

Greenwood also talks about the Christian belief in the Trinity, where differences have to be accepted for what they are: 'Unity is not to be equated with the denial of difference or the reduction of them all to one, but speaks of the mutual intercommunion and interpenetration of elements of difference.'[2]

So if we want to love and be loved, we have to be ourselves in such a way that we also allow others the freedom to be themselves.

Accepting that life moves on

But if we are going to achieve all this, we have to be very secure within ourselves in our relationship with God. Otherwise, how are we to maintain our personal integrity in an institution that at times threatens to take away our identity? How do we hold on to the life of God within us?

Going back means that we have to accept that life moves on. Things are not going to be the same ever again. Going back means that we have to love others enough to allow them to change too, or not change if they do not want to or are unable to. And despite their sameness or difference we have to have the security to be who we have become.

I am reminded of a time recently when I had to read a short paper in the presence of a learned academic who had been the examiner of a research thesis I had once put together. Years had elapsed between the two meetings and I had moved on a great deal. Yet, although he was gracious, I had to work hard not to feel intimidated and adopt my previous role of student.

There are those who have the same problem when,

having left home, they return to visit their parents. We sometimes have to struggle to maintain our adult identity and new role in the family over against the expectations of our parents who continue to treat us as young children.

Wrestling with whom?

So we return to Jacob's story and his wrestling at Peniel. Exactly whom he wrestled with is a matter for debate. The Bible text we are given says that he fought with a man; it was only afterwards that Jacob came to the conclusion that he had come face to face with God and had survived.

The rabbinical accounts reveal a variety of opinions. Some say the other person was a shepherd or a sage, although the majority see him as an angel.[3] Once the idea that he was an angel had been accepted the Midrash tried to identify him. But which angel? Was he Esau's angel or might he have been Jacob's angel? We will have our own ideas about this although it is interesting for us to note here that there are those who think that this man with whom Jacob wrestled was his guardian angel or more specifically the other half of himself.[4]

So this is the story not of a human being fighting an angel or God-like being in natural/supernatural combat. It is, rather, a story of Jacob's inner wrestling. It is about his own inner struggle as he fights to achieve the final process of the reinvention of himself. This final phase involves his coming to terms with his identity as the necessary prelude to his act of reconciliation. This is to be followed by his reintegration into his family and homeland. In losing his false identity as defined by others, he discovers his authentic self as being grounded in God.

When it is understood in this way, Jacob's journey is no longer about supernatural other-worldly combat. It has a more down-to-earth significance. It now becomes much more consonant with similar journeys that we might be making today.

Looking a little closer at the text, we note first of all that this event took place at night. Having already seen how the epiphany at Bethel took place at night, we are left with the impression that God is most active in the forming of Jacob's vocation during the hours of darkness.

Many of us no doubt will testify that it has been through the darkest times of our ministry when we have learned the most. This is true for those engaged in lay ministry, too. Paradoxically, again, we can discover that in his apparent absence God is most present.

Winter and waiting

St Isaac the Syrian reminds us that the times of darkness and death are to be regarded as winter rather than as some kind of extinction. In winter we need to remember that 'the seeds lie deep within the earth, waiting for spring, when they put out new shoots'.[5] He writes:

> How blessed is the person who, out of hope for God's grace, has endured the dejectedness which is a hidden trial of the mind's virtue and growth. It is like the gloom of winter, which nevertheless causes the hidden seed to grow as it disintegrates under the ground in the harsh changes of blustery weather.[6]

Speaking for myself, I cannot be anything other than positive and hopeful – most of the time – concerning the future of our church. I feel we are in a time of revolution. It is as if God has finally brought the Church of England to its knees by financial crisis, all other recent attempts having failed.

I should add that I call it a time of 'revolution' rather than the more popular 'reformation' because I perceive that the latter term today means to some simply a re-branding or reorganizing of what we are already doing. A 'revolution' on the other hand will rescue us from unhelpful tradition and place creative love once more at the centre of our daily being and becoming. Here we can discover ourselves simultaneously in touch with the earth and heaven.

It is a sad reflection on our spiritual life then that few will admit to what is really going on. We bring about changes to our way of life that are clearly finance-driven and yet we try and put a layer of theological respectability over them to pretend they are something else. The tragedy will be that if we refuse at all costs to admit to the patient's terminal illness, and fail to face up to our grief, we will not be able to move on in any really meaningful way.

Why cannot those who insist on using the term 'reformation' admit at least that we have been over-indulgent in promoting the interests of the establishment so that institutional matters have mattered more than the demands of Divine love?

Only when we are prepared to be radical and take big risks in our response to the challenges that face us today, can we look forward to being members of a healthier, fitter, more vibrant church.

When, however, we insist on trying to prop up what we've got – if our reaction consists of nothing more than palliative care – then we are going to have to face up to the dreadful truth that both what we love and what we are growing into will die.

Darkness is not to be shunned but welcomed.

But what was it about his inner self that Jacob had to come to terms with?

Holding on to who I am

Was it his conscience, his fear, or a feeling of isolation? Perhaps this wrestling in the darkness was Jacob's Gethsemane prayer. Here, at this place and point of time apparently chosen by God, his will had to fight and eventually submit to the will of God.

Part of him yearned for the security and power that came from enjoying the rewards of his good husbandry. He had worked hard and earned everything he had. Why shouldn't he enjoy it in comfort rather than moving to a place where he might lose everything including his life? Happily, Jacob worked through these questions so that the Divine purpose for his life took precedence over his desire for a petty self-centred existence. Significantly, it was because he chose this path that in the days and years to come a nation would arise that would bear the name of Israel. Aligning ourselves with the purposes of God – 'thy will and not my will' – rather than those purposes of humanity that deny us our identity, is how we progress from dust to divinity.

This unity of will brings us back to our need for humility which is, as I have said, both the start and an intrinsic central feature of Christian holiness.

The author of The Cloud of Unknowing differentiates between imperfect and perfect humility. Imperfect humility 'springs from mixed motives, even if God is the chief reason'. Perfect humility 'is caused solely by God'. And true humility is 'nothing else but a true knowledge and awareness of oneself as one really is. For surely whoever truly saw and felt himself as he is, would truly be humble.' The author goes on to say, 'therefore strain every nerve in every possible way to know and experience yourself as you really are'.[7]

The fruit of the Spirit-filled life here depends upon the way in which we allow the Holy Spirit to get to work on our inner identities. It is about an inward transformation that forges a new relationship between ourselves and others and the world in which we live.

This can be seen in the way the New Testament speaks of holiness in terms of life in the Spirit rather than defining it by particular rituals or holiness codes. Holiness in the New Covenant is understood in terms of union with the world rather than separation.

By contrast, in the Old Testament, holiness as we first come across it describes a place of meeting: 'The place is awesome, glorious, terrifying, mysterious and compelling. Holiness is marked by fear and awe.'[8]

So we may understand that at Peniel Jacob was wrestling to accept his true identity. His future life held no meaning for him unless it was grounded in God. If holiness is about the union between God and ourselves then we have to be grounded in God in such a way that we have no illusions either about our strengths or our weaknesses.

If we pursue the idea of vocation in the context of personal development, we have to admit that there comes a time – at least once – when we, too, have to meet and wrestle with ourselves. Sometimes we can find ourselves in situations where we have to struggle with our inner desires. These are often to do with unhelpful and inhibiting experiences from the past that seem to exert their own power to try and determine how we are to live in the present. We can, of course, refuse to wrestle and simply give in to them. If we do, our lives and ministry will go on but they will probably be to some degree impoverished. When we are prepared to take our inner desires on, we are likely to discover that it is in the night time that God is most active and that it is in powerlessness and brokenness that we discover the meaning and purpose that makes sense of the mess.

When we sense a freedom from these desires, we can be almost overcome by feelings of awe and fear at the wonder and mystery of the God who gives us life and who can give us back our freedom to be ourselves when others have enslaved us. Jacob feels like this at Bethel where he also senses the comforting presence of God. He finds it again later on at Peniel when he is asked to surrender any final desire to live his life to some degree or other in the past.

In the face of the challenges that lay ahead, Jacob quite naturally looked back to the security he had known before. There was a safety to be had from familiar surroundings. But now it was a place that could only offer him the restrictions of childhood dependency. Yet he was also aware that a return to the earlier stages of grief, although painful, offered some kind of refuge from having to grow up again. But if he returned he feared he would lose both himself and his growing faith in God. In finding his identity he would have to face the rather terrifying truth that God was after all the ground of his being.

To be specific, Jacob is wrestling with the person he had lost. Not only is it tempting to become his old self again but, as we have seen, he is particularly afraid that in meeting Esau he will revert to being the person he was before he had left home. And he fears being caught up again in the arguments and alienation that he had put behind him. Going back, therefore, seems a price too high to pay. He cannot go back like that any more than he can deny the person he has become through the intervening years.

So the old Jacob is here again, exerting an influence, threatening to suffocate the freedom and fullness of life the new Jacob has worked so hard to find. This is the old Jacob who was trapped by tradition, the person whose identity had been defined by what others had determined was right to do or not do. This was a Jacob whose degree of self-denial put holiness out of reach.

But this, of course, is a story with a happy ending. Jacob wrestles and wins through. He does not win over God but with God he wins through and establishes his new identity while his old self slips quietly and namelessly away. God after all has not only been working through this breaking process, he has been in it. In the departure of the former self there is a blessing defined by a dislocated hip. This was a symbol both of Jacob's need to depend upon God at all times in the future and his need to remain firmly, heavily, in touch with the earth.

So we should not be surprised that when we reach this level of self-understanding and self-determination by Divine process we, too, can find God in ourselves and ourselves in God. Frightening though it sounds, we find eternity in this fullness of life which cannot be bought and which belongs only to the kingdom of God rather than the many and diverse kingdoms in this world.

The final farewell

This leads us to consider *the fourth and final task of grief*, which is part of the process involved in healing pain. This includes the ability to say a final farewell to the cause of our grief so that we can make fresh attachments; so that we can reinvest our emotional energy in new relationships and in new ways.

We need to be able to achieve some kind of healthy distance between ourselves and what we have lost without feeling guilt, anger or bitterness any more. Residual grief arising from our memories will remain but this can be accommodated and managed in such a way that it is no longer dominant in our life. While residual grief is natural, and it is healthy to revisit it at times, it is not something that can shake our lives off course any more.

Jacob experienced two 'deaths' and two bereavements when he first left home. First, in walking away from the tradition that reduced him to the status of a child, and, second, when he stopped being the person he had become as a result of living under the yoke of that tradition.

With the sunrise at Peniel, Jacob has worked through his grief to such an extent that he is able to turn his back on these deaths and the power they have had over him. Although he is now working more than ever from a place of pain and weakness, he is able to face the future with hope. At long last, it is now possible for him to fulfil God's purpose for his life.

So, as he works through this fourth task he finds that he is 'gaining a new and often stronger and more intense life despite recurring pain' from the losses he has suffered.[9]

The ordained minister today, assessing his or her role in a parish – given the changing nature of ministry and the evolving structures of the church – is also likely to be called to confront not only the prospect of departure, prayer in the night and a new relationship with the community, but also the need to reinvent and reinvest the self into the working out of his or her vocation anew.

This will involve wrestling with those other ways we have of being ourselves, the life-denying ways in which we go about our service of others; the ways in which we work out our vocation that deny our identity. We have to struggle loose from the overpowering traditions we inherit when we 'turn our collars around' and others address us as 'Reverend', as well as breaking free from a host of unreasonable expectations. Instead of seeking respectability at all costs, we learn to respect ourselves as people in whom God has invested so much of himself.

This sounds like hard work. It certainly demands from us a great deal of honesty and courage. But we are already aware from other aspects of church life that there are no easy or quick solutions to the challenges we face. Yet, relating the four tasks of grief to spiritual growth as I have suggested can provide us with a way of becoming dependent upon our earthiness at the same time as discovering our divinity.

Unable to walk properly by our own strength any more, we rely heavily on the earth to support us while learning increasingly to become ourselves. We can now recognize Christ in ourselves in a humble and not a haughty manner, and also see and share him with others.

In saying goodbye to the models of priesthood that are based upon power and position within a hierarchical tradition, we are able to say hello to a new way into vocational holiness. By turning the priorities of the world and many of the prevailing traditions of the church upside down, we can limp away from hierarchical power structures and rejoice in a humility and holiness that is more consonant with the life of Christ.

This is the Christ we have received through Scripture and that other tradition that helps rather than hinders us and which was followed with such effect in the very early days of the church.

The wounded healer

The most prominent feature associated with vocational holiness is the humility of the life of the incarnate Christ within the minister. For we have not been called to model the kind of ministry that is likely to reduce others to the status of children. Having escaped it ourselves, it would be unfair to inflict it on others. The holiness we seek to have and share should promote the spiritual well-being and becoming of others.

Henri Nouwen in his writing on the wounded healer says:

It is not the task of the Christian leader to go around nervously trying to redeem people, to save them at the last

minute, to put them on the right track. For we are re-
deemed once and for all. The Christian leader is called to
help others affirm this great news, and to make visible in
daily events the fact that behind the dirty curtain of our
painful symptoms there is something great to be seen: the
face of Him in whose image we are shaped.[10]

In this sense, all those who pursue a vocation within the
church community should, metaphorically speaking, walk
to some degree or other with a limp. And we should not be
ashamed to do so. Without parading our wounds for public affirmation, the fulfilment of our vocation can be greatly
enhanced when our wounds – or rather their effect – become apparent to others. These wounds – dare I say it – are
the wounds of the rejected and unfulfilled love of Christ.
These wounds are supposed to bring healing to others.

This is in stark contrast to that other understanding of
ministry which tries subconsciously to measure and match
us up to the wholly Otherness of God or to a mistaken understanding of the perfection of Christ. All such attempts
are fruitless because perfection in the gospel is to do with
finding our place and fulfilling our potential rather than
claiming any degree of faultlessness.

I gave up any desire to be good long ago. I recognize that
I am flawed, but thanks to the indwelling Spirit of God, not
fatally so. I am a sinner – like anyone else, maybe more so
– yet I live in the presence of God by the grace of God. I
have not earned any merit by being any less sinful than I
was before. But I have grown closer to God as I have grown
up and taken responsibility for my life with him.

I have rejected any kind of religious system that reduces
me to the status of child-like dependence as being unhelpful
for my growth into emotional and spiritual adulthood. I am
released from the drives of religious conformity, which so
often come from the need of those either within religious

structures or those outside who use them for their own ends in the search for power over others.

Metropolitan Anthony, when writing about the holiness of prayer, says that God does sometimes escape us,

> not because we do not look for Him but because we look for Him everywhere where He is not. From this point of view Bonhoeffer is with us when he says that Christianity is a religion without religion, if we understand by the word 'religion' a system of methods that make it possible to catch God, to take Him captive, to get Him in a trap and keep Him there. Yes, in this case Christianity, and only Christianity, is a religion without a religion, because God wanted to make Himself interior to our condition, and He wanted us to have no need to try to hold Him captive, Who became flesh in order to be with us. There is no need for us to try to use methods and techniques to make Him our prisoner.[11]

This leads me to share a time in my own life when, having read and preached about it for years, I seemed suddenly to stumble across the kingdom of God in this world. This was one among other powerful experiences that helped me re-discover the meaning of my vocation in terms of the model of the wounded healer.

About five years ago, I unexpectedly found myself lying on a trolley in the accident and emergency department of my local hospital. I was in shock and great pain and unable to move at all. For a while I thought I was going to die. Others did, too. I was told that if I pulled through, I was likely to be confined to a wheelchair and unable to function at all from the waist down.

Happily, following major surgery, I was eventually dis-charged from hospital and began the long haul back to health. I was living on my own at the time, but Valerie, my secretary, was wonderful in the way she looked after and supported me during my convalescence. While I was still recovering slowly, my diocesan bishop sent me to a nursing home where I was looked after for a while by an Augustinian order of nursing sisters.[12]

It was winter and the days were short, and while I only stayed for a week it was in this unlikely situation that I made the most profound discovery that would change my understanding of ministry for good.

As well as being in pain, I also felt depressed to such an extent that I began to wonder whether or not I was going mad.

There were other patients in this nursing home who were also suffering from physical and some from psychological ailments. Here there were no locks on the doors and no privacy. I began to wonder whether I had been sent to some kind of institution for the mentally ill.

I wondered whether I was being led into insanity so that I might discover true sanity. Was I crazy? It wasn't for me to say but if others didn't tell me, how would I ever know whether I was sane or not?

I wondered how much further I would have to sink before I began to come up. It crossed my mind that I might stay at the bottom of this dark pit and never surface again. Had I been taking everything too seriously? My work and my concerns about the welfare of others? As a Christian, and particularly as a priest, I thought I should be able to cope with misfortune better than this. I had spent years believing and praying but I didn't feel holy at all. I was just a pathetic, weak shell of my former energetic and active self. Humility at this point for me had become compulsory.

I wrote in my journal:

Yesterday, one of the 'inmates' – an eighty-six-year-old lady who says she is still a young person trapped in the failing body of someone much older – told me that the advice I had given her a few days ago about how to get rid of cramp had worked. She is a lovely person. She gets a lot of cramp, which she finds very painful, particularly when she is lying in bed. She was so grateful for my remedy and I was immensely pleased to have been able to help.

I am sure there is something of deeper meaning here. It has to do with the kind of help I can offer others now.

I was shocked the first time I saw us all – the patients in this nursing home – making our way down the long corridors of this vast converted house towards the dining room. It is a sight that is repeated every time we have a meal.

The gong goes and out of the shadows emerge these broken, bruised and bowed figures from every direction. It takes us ages – as if in slow motion – as we shuffle and stagger and struggle our way towards the meal table. The blind, the crippled, the lame and the maimed. To sit at some messy messianic banquet.

I am reminded of the parable of the great feast in Luke (Luke 14.5–23). The power-mongers make their excuses. Their ambition is the acquisition of more power, which, they believe, gives them the right to continue to exert unhealthy influence over the lives of others. Western society seems to worship power. Success for many is understood in terms of securing a greater income than they need and a position which makes them feel superior. In our weakness, they would only see abject failure.

Those who pursue the latest innovation that is supposed to make life easier are elsewhere. They think that time-saving, labour-efficient technology is the answer when all that it does is help you spin the wheel faster. It is not surprising they are not here. How can anyone develop a spiritual life and get to know God when they don't have the time to be still? So they bypass this inefficient and unproductive band of losers.

Those who love but keep that love largely to themselves are absent, too. They have interpreted love principally as something that is cosy and comfortable. But authentic love has more to do with contract and commitment. It is about committing oneself to the good of others and not deserting them when they let us down. That is what is meant by the covenant – or contract – love of God. In God's love, while there is warmth, there is also a fire that burns against the injustice that stunts human growth and development. This is not a love you can keep for yourself at home. There are those who are afraid to share this love with the likes of us for fear of losing what they've got. They don't realise that they've lost it already.

So who is left who will attend this banquet? Who do the roads and lanes throw up?

Well, there is this unlikely little band of battered people, thrown together in their brokenness. We have two things in common: faith in God and a painful awareness of our sickness. We are from all walks of life and from all over the country. We've not come voluntarily but at the Lord's bidding. We never thought this was a table that we would ever sit at. Quite simply, we have been blessed by our sickness for only now do we understand that we share a vocation to sit at a common meal. But no ordinary meal is this, for Christ is present here. We have not earned the right to sit here. We are too weak and feeble for that. We are here by grace. And grace alone. In our need and because we have faith, we have been called.

So around this table there is no rejoicing that we have made it 'in' while ignoring the plight of those who are 'out'. Instead, there is a quiet acceptance of where we are and an enormous sense of gratitude towards our companions.

I feel that by helping the old lady with cramp in the way that I did, I have passed on a greater good, enabled the growth of love and extended the kingdom of God more than I would previously have thought I could. Previously I had relied on clever sermons and so-called spiritual talks that probably weren't very spiritual at all. But here in this institution, I realise that I am nothing. Here I have nothing to give.

And yet, how can there be such great spiritual significance in so small an act? It is not in the act itself, clearly. Nor even is it the amount of love in the act. For that would make me proud about my ability to make others feel better. The significance has to do with the place from which love comes. Now I have been pulled down from the heights of my false piety, I find reality in another's pain.

Here *I* am eighty-six years old and suffering from cramp. Here I am part of the others I am with. But here Christ is in us all. We are one Body. Broken, battered, bruised and bleeding. Yet one body bound together by Christ. Here I am nobody and yet I am everybody. While I have nothing of myself to give, I share the love of God.

Now I can understand why Jesus broke the bread before he gave it. Now I can see a new significance in the repetition of this act in the service of Holy Communion. He wasn't merely showing us how he was prepared to be broken for us. He broke the bread in anticipation of our brokenness for him. Because it is by our brokenness that we find Christ who is himself broken. And once we have found him we are bound up and built up. In the healing of our wounds we become stronger.

Hitherto, I bore the hallmarks of all three groups of people in the gospel story who were absent from the banquet. So much of my Christian life was bound up with the exercise of power. Being fit and healthy, able to cope with endless pressure, able to be all things to all people, not being angry, being 'successful' in personal relationships. In other words, not being true to myself. This was neither the power that Christ embodied nor the power that he called his Church to have.

As a parish priest, I assumed power in the management of others. I was the managing director. Apart from any personal desire to have my own way, others expected me to be a leader in this mould. I led. They followed. But when Jesus invited others to follow him, he spent most of his time asking them questions rather than giving them answers. That is why those who believed him were given power to believe in themselves (John 1.12).

Power that belittles others is not of God. For the power of servanthood releases rather than restricts God's life in others. No wonder I find the pursuit of holiness elusive. I've wasted too much time already in the pursuit of a power that doesn't exist within the kingdom of God. This can only be another of those reasons why the church looks like any other human institution. Small wonder others find it unattractive. Instead of offering a way of being released to enjoy a fuller life, it invites self-condemnation and imposes more rules that restrict personal development.

I still don't sleep well nor do I find myself relaxing. I feel most of all here an encounter with desolation. No longer surrounded by the busyness of life, I am being made to focus on its beauty in the most simple and unlikely things. In a handful of soil rather than in a mountain range.

When I leave here I shall not be healed in the sense of having solved all my problems. I may leave here and die. I will walk with some difficulty and often in pain but I shall be healed in another and more complete way. While I shall struggle to lift my feet off the ground, and even though my body will still hurt and I shall continue to struggle in my spiritual journey, for the first time in my life I shall feel whole and content.

So while I have looked and searched in vain for it for so long and in so many places, in this place and through this brokenness, I find that I have inadvertently stumbled across the kingdom. Here there is a kingdom not of this world. Here the priorities of the world are stood on their head.

Here reality is neither about power or success nor even about love. For what do I really know about true love that is free of the instincts of self-preservation? All I know about now is the love of God. And yet it is not even about love. It is about grace. About the welcome and acceptance God has for us. It is about a retreat from the world of power and possessions and a greater immersion into inner reality. It is about the fusion of Spirit and matter. Breath and dust. It is about the life ahead in the here and now.

This extract from my journal reminds me most of all that when human identity and meaning meet together in such a powerful way, life can never be the same again. We all, no doubt, have had similar experiences when heaven and earth seemed to unite. When our faith grows cold, we need to remind ourselves of these powerful experiences when we catch sight of that kingdom which lies within us all. When we revisit these memories and sometimes touch the scars that we bear from former times, we can quickly find ourselves once more gazing into the face of God.

Later on in his life, when Jacob's family had 'taken on foreign gods', God told him to take his family back to Bethel where they would be purified and the promises of faith would be renewed (Genesis 35.1–13). When the time of purification was complete, they moved on again. So going back is not always bad news. Sometimes, by retracing our steps we can retrieve our promised redemption.

So, like Jacob, it is important that if we are to move away from a system that enslaves us in order to re-enter it later on, we need to avoid adopting our old identity under the pressure to conform that comes from many different sources. We need to remember where we have come from and who we have become. We need to have our true identity confirmed by God by returning to the earth and grounding ourselves in humility. *Adam* makes most sense when in touch with *adamah*.

It may well be, therefore, that the difficult times we are going through now represent our best opportunity to fulfil our vocation. While we might only make a journey like Jacob's once in our ministry, the way we handle ourselves along the way is all-important.

We can try and ignore the difficulties or walk away from them thereby denying ourselves the opportunity to learn from them. Or we can misunderstand them and see them only as a cause for regret or shame or guilt. Or we can forever protest our innocence and instead of permitting the pain to purify us, we can nurse our wounds in ever-increasing degrees of bitterness. Or we can accept them, embrace them and be transformed by them.

Archimandrite Sophrony was born in Russia in 1896. After the October Revolution he lived and worked in Paris as an artist. However, to find his true identity, he moved to Mount Athos and became a monk. Here his spiritual guide was Staretz Silouan. He later returned to France where he published the writing of St Silouan, which had been entrusted to him. However, because of severe illness, he was unable to return to Athos and moved to England where he eventually died. His journey therefore was not dissimilar to Jacob's.

In contrast to our career-mindedness and concern with

the preservation of religious respectability, Sophrony writes that our birthright is none other than divinization by the Holy Spirit. Without this we are nothing.

> The Lord justified and hallowed His forefathers in the flesh. Likewise each one of us, if we follow Christ's commandments, can with tears of repentance restore the Divine Image in ourselves, which is clouded over, and thereby justify ourselves in our personal being, and assist in the justification of the generations that preceded us. We all of us bear within ourselves the fate of all mankind: it goes beyond the bounds of earthly history and changes the course of cosmic life, for the world was created from such beings. When for the sake of a 'pottage of lentils' (Gen. 25.33–34) people refuse the path indicated by Christ – divinisation by the power of the Holy Spirit and the adoption of sons to the Eternal father – the whole point of man's appearance in the world vanishes.[13]

Whatever happens, I don't think that as priests in pursuit of a holy life we can avoid these times when we are broken. Nor do I think we should deny their significance. Instead, we should not be surprised when they come along.

One of the most important verses of the New Testament for our understanding of Christian ministry and priestly vocation in particular is the one about the dying seed: 'Very truly, I tell you, unless a grain of wheat falls into the earth and dies, it remains just a single grain; but if it dies, it bears much fruit' (John 12.24). While in itself it may have been simply a reference to the resurrection, it reminds us of the need to be prepared to die and rise again if we wish to become effective witnesses to the truth of healing love.

It is only when we have been taken from our position of safety, and have experienced the freezing temperatures of the spiritual chill of our times, that we can begin to realize that it is only here, as the life of God thrusts upwards and outwards relentlessly from within, that authentic, sacrificial love comes to the surface. What is more, we have to be prepared to experience this through as many winters as God deems it will take for the eventual harvest to be as plentiful as possible.[14]

So when we feel troubled and under siege we might profitably ask ourselves whether this is not some way in which we are being reminded of the need to be ourselves. It may be that we have begun to adopt again our old styles of behaviour. Once we have made the journey, it is helpful for us from time to time to ask ourselves whether – either by collusion or by over-independence and a desire to assert our rights – we are subconsciously becoming conformed again to that tradition that enslaved us?

Being down to earth with God

Brokenness properly welcomed involves the replacement of self-centredness with God-centredness. It makes more room for the life of the Spirit to confer divinity to bless and transform our humanity. It can also bring us back down to earth with a bump when we have been moving away from the gravity of God.

While, however, it seems that we are more likely to come across the kingdom in these trying circumstances than anywhere else, it is not all hard work and bad news.

For here there is a peace and a depth of contentment and joy that are to be had as the result of the operation of the Divine *ruach* or Spirit upon our lives and souls as we begin to learn how to breathe in time with God. Jesus is not simply providing comfort for his followers in times of difficulty when he says, 'Come to me, all you that are weary and are carrying heavy burdens, and I will give you rest. Take my yoke upon you, and learn from me; for I am gentle and humble in heart, and you will find rest for your souls. For my yoke is easy, and my burden is light' (Matthew 11.28–30). There is more than comfort here. This is a revelation of the nature of God as it operates within human nature.

This moves us away from our any over-reliance upon our understanding of an interventionist God that reduces us to a state of frustrated faithlessness by God's apparent inactivity and unconcern over our suffering. Jesus here speaks more in terms of Divine and human co-operation in both the suffering and joy of redemption.

Our humility therefore finds its source and meaning in the humility of the heart of God. Jesus says that God is 'gentle and humble in heart'; his incarnation means that God can be down to earth, too. Not confined by the earth but down to earth with you and me.

This is why the crucifixion is such a powerful image of humanity's denial of God. God wants to be down to earth, but in our rejection of Christ we lifted him up and hanged him on a cross, suspending him above the earth.

His Divine interference with our day-to-day life was neither welcome nor appreciated by a religion that preferred to keep God at a distance where it was easier to define and distribute his presence and power.

But is it possible – are we being reasonable – to suggest that we might model this kind of humility and holiness both within the church and to the world? Or is this something that you can write about and read but forget as soon as you make contact with others? Can we really hang on to these ideals – or any other ideals of service and humility in prayer and holiness – either by collusion or by over-independence and a desire to assert our rights within the parish system which we have at the present? Did we not largely lose this identity gradually over the years as we got to grips with parish ministry? Wasn't it inevitable that our dreams should give way to harsh reality? Can we really hold on to the priestly identity we secretly long to have, express, share and surrender to God?

If our response to this is to say 'no' then we have come to the conclusion that the life of holiness is confined to others, maybe to those who are members of religious orders and others who may not have the institutional distractions that we have to contend with. To say 'no' is to affirm that the leaders of the church have finally become managers and administrators, fundraisers and pastoral counsellors rather than spiritual leaders. To say 'no' is to deny the church the room the Holy Spirit needs in order to breathe new life both into ourselves and into those we seek to serve.

On the other hand we may want to say that, while it is extremely difficult, we can – we must – hold on to our priestly identity, our calling to be people of prayer in the midst of a community of prayer. And it is only when we do hold on and rediscover that identity that we will be able to restore some spiritual credibility to our interpretation of the gospel.

This will entail reviewing our working life, and from the list of things that we do, eliminating those that do not fall within the pattern of this calling. To do so may cause unease, dismay and even a certain amount of chaos among others. But this again is one of the tasks of grief that we are working through and which others have to work through as well.

I say again, there is no future in palliative care. Nor is there any future in a more professional clergy and a more efficiently and better organized church without the humility that is the hallmark of the holiness of our vocation.

I rather fancy that even after his reconciliation with his brother and his life that followed, Jacob was forced on occasion to wrestle in his mind – if not through his prayers – with other maybe slightly different causes of frustration when the wrong kind of tradition caught up with him again. If he did, then every time he emerged from these encounters, he will have been reaffirmed in his calling, identity and destiny.

Following a retreat of mind and spirit, as we re-enter the structures that have caused us so much pain, we, too, can revisit the place from which we derive our identity as many times as we need to. We have been given the gift of prayer and it is expected that our prayer life will be central to who we are with God and with others.

Yet how many of us can put our hands on our hearts and say that we pray as much as we would like to? I once heard a celebrity being asked what he would have written on his tombstone. His reply was, 'I wish I had prayed more.' I have a dread of having to repeat those words myself one day.

But without this commitment to prayer, humility and the pursuit of holiness, our vocation – and the vocations of others which we foster – lose their meaning.

When moving away makes sense

I would like to make one final observation. There are times in the pursuit of a holy life and in obedience to the Holy Spirit, when, having tried to reinvest ourselves within a community, we find we cannot resist the temptations of returning to being the ungrounded people we once were. So with reluctance we have no alternative but to settle elsewhere.

When this happens, it is not an indication of the failure of our vocation. It is more likely that our need to move on proves how hard the way has been and how exhausted we have become.

So, very occasionally, even though we have been through the journey and have wrestled with and left behind the person and the place where we were, the risks of slipping back into our old ways are so great that it is right – although usually in very exceptional cases – to move on. In order for this God-breathed dust which is me to retain its hope, there may be occasions when I have to shake the dust of other people's lives from my feet so that I may journey on unencumbered by the clutter of broken and unworkable relationships. If I do, I can find the opportunity to start again and express my vocation afresh in new circumstances.

St Francis did not return to the home he so famously left. He remained away and outside in the countryside. But this did not result in his annihilation. He rebuilt the church of San Damiano and went on to rebuild the medieval church. Sometimes in the fourth task of grief we find it more than we can do to say goodbye to past dreams. Returning to the same locality will reignite both their passion and their power and we will not be able to reinvest our energy in new ways. Instead of moving on, we will come to a standstill.

After Jesus healed the blind man outside Bethsaida, he ordered him not to return to the village but to go home. I rather think that this man was not evil – he was brought to Jesus by his friends – but that he had given himself to unhelpful relationships with such intensity that he had become confused, even bewildered, by them. This had happened to such a degree that he had become blind to the intrinsic worth and identity of others. That is why when Jesus restored his sight, the man recognizes people only partially. To begin with they look like trees, and then with further healing he begins to see clearly again and recognize people for who they really are.

Maybe this man had given himself sacrificially to others but had become so hurt or so tired that he ended up treating them with less respect than he should have. We don't have to be evil or even bad people to do this. Just hurt or tired to the extent that the pain overwhelms our humility and as a consequence our ability to see and serve Christ in others.

When the pain and frustration get to us we can end up dividing others into two groups: those whom we accept because they seem to understand and sympathize with our predicament and those we dismiss because they do not or will not understand. This second group might as well be trees, for all the understanding and acceptance we give them.

So as the layers of self-deception were removed, we can guess that the blind man could see that his human relationships had gone seriously wrong. After Jesus prays with him a second time we read that 'he saw everything clearly'. Or should we say, 'he saw everyone clearly'.

Jesus therefore tells the man not to return to the village. To do so would mean that he would become hopelessly entangled again by all the old problems and entwined in fruitless relationships. Jesus knew that the man was not strong enough to fight these influences on his own.

There is no condemnation here but simply a recognition that the only way forward for him involved turning his back on where he had been. He had to go to a home where he could feel safe and secure, to recover his strength and spiritual insight so that one day he might set out once again.

Again it is worth reminding ourselves that while Jacob returned first of all to be once again with his brother Esau, it was not long before they moved on in their separate directions, Esau returning to Seir and Jacob moving on to Succoth and from there to Shechem (Genesis 33.17–18).

God was never far from Jacob. Wherever he went, he was never alone. It is the same for all pilgrims. And it is just as true for those who embark on the journey of priesthood. Along this way there is nothing that can separate us from God, not even the death of those we hold most dear or even the death of ourselves. For in darkness there is light and in death there is life.

It is in the light and life of Christ that we may understand afresh the words, 'Blessed are those who mourn, for they will be comforted' (Matthew 5.4).

A Prayer for Humility

Lord, unless you bless me
I shall not remain
in touch with this earth
into which you breathed
your destiny.

For this God-breathed 'me'
is no ordinary dust
but Spirit and matter
fashioned to embrace
eternity.

Not just for me: for others too
when down to earth and in touch with heaven
we discover
death and resurrection
simultaneously.

Gathering precious dust
from all over the world
dear God of Divine story
make sense
of us.

A.C.

NOTES

Introduction

1 For this I have used a description of these four tasks given in the book *Healing Pain* by Nini Leick and Marianne Davidson-Nielson (Routledge, 1991, pp. 25–63). For a more in-depth consideration of the theory underpinning the practice they describe, it is worth referring to J. William Worden, *Grief Counselling and Grief Therapy* (Routledge, 1991, 2nd edn).

1 Called or Culled?

1 Iris Murdoch, *The Black Prince* (Vintage, 1999), p. 238.

2 Alvin Toffler, *Future Shock* (New York: Pan Books, 1970), referred to by Gerard Kelly, *Get a Grip on the Future* (Monarch Books, 1999), p. 28.

3 Andrew Clitherow, *Into Your Hands* (SPCK, 2001), pp. 81–2.

4 John Tiller, *A Strategy for the Church's Ministry* (CIO Publishing, 1983), pp. 97–100.

5 Alan Kreider, *Worship and Evangelism in Pre-Christendom*, Grove Booklet no. 32 (Grove Books, 1995), p. 12.

6 *Epistle to Diognetus*, to be found for example in *The Teachings of the Church Fathers* by John R. Willis SJ (San Francisco: Ignatius Press, 2002), p. 38.

7 Kreider, *Worship and Evangelism*, p. 40.

8 David Runcorn, *Holiness*, Grove Booklet no. 54 (Grove Books, 1995), p. 14.

9 Francis Dewar, *Called or Collared?* (SPCK, 2000), p. 13. The title of this chapter is of course a parody on the title of Dewar's book.

2 Prayer in the Night

1 Christina Rossetti, 'Hope in Grief', from *Poems and Prose: Christina Rossetti*, ed. Jan Marsh (Everyman, 1994), p. 5.

2 Dietrich Bonhoeffer, *The Cost of Discipleship* (SCM Press, 1959), p. 86.

3 Thomas J. McGovern, *Priestly Identity* (Four Courts Press, 2002), p. 126.

4 From *Presbyterorum ordinis*, quoted in McGovern, *Priestly Identity*, pp. 126–7.

5 See Alexander Ryrie, *Silent Waiting* (Canterbury Press, 1999), p. 17.

6 Ignatius of Loyola, *Personal Writings* (Penguin Books, 1996), Annotations 314–324, pp. 348–9; Annotations 329–336, pp. 351–3.

7 Ignatius of Loyola, *Personal Writings*, Letter 4, pp. 132–3.

8 Ignatius of Loyola, *Personal Writings*, Annotations 314–324, pp. 348–9.

9 *Common Worship: Services and Prayers for the Church of England*, Eucharistic Prayer G, © The Archbishops' Council 2000.

10 Simone Weil, *Waiting on God* (New York: Harper & Row, 1973), p. x, quoted by J. Neville Ward in *The Use of Praying* (Epworth Press, 1968), p. 139.

11 Michael Ramsey, *The Christian Priest Today* (SPCK, 1999), p. 14.

12 Ramsey, *The Christian Priest Today*, p. 17.

13 Rowan Williams, *Lost Icons* (Continuum, 2000), p. 224.

14 In 1986 plans were put in place to rebuild the church. A restoration committee chaired by the then Archdeacon of Montgomery, the Ven. W. T. Pritchard was appointed and the Revd Paul Davies was licensed as priest-in-charge in 1988. He and his wife worked tirelessly to make Pennant Melangell a centre for prayer and healing. The restoration was completed in 1992. Today the Revd Evelyn Davies serves two parishes based on Aberdaron on the Llyn peninsula.

15 St Bernard, *The Steps of Humility* (The Saint Austin Press, 2001), p. 27.

16 St Bernard, *The Steps of Humility*, p. 32.

3 *Walking Wounded*

1 Robin Greenwood, *Transforming Priesthood: A New Theology of Mission and Ministry* (SPCK, 1994), p. 90.

2 Greenwood, *Transforming Priesthood*, p. 88.

3 Elie Wiesel, *Messengers of God* (Touchstone, 1994), p. 123.

4 Wiesel, *Messengers of God*, p. 124.

5 Hilarion Alfeyev, *The Spiritual World of Isaac the Syrian* (Cistercian Publications, 2000), p. 107. St Isaac, also known as Isaac of Nineveh, wrote in the seventh century.

6 Alfeyev, *Isaac*, p. 107.

7 *The Cloud of Unknowing and Other Works* (Penguin Books, 1961), p. 79.

8 David Runcorn, *Holiness*, Grove Booklet no. 54 (Grove Books, 1995), p. 6.

9 Nini Leick and Marianne Davidson-Nielsen, *Healing Pain* (Routledge, 1991), pp. 59–63.

10 Henri Nouwen, *The Wounded Healer* (Image Books, 1979), p. 44.

11 Metropolitan Anthony of Sourozh, *The Essence of Prayer* (Darton, Longman & Todd, 1986), p. 306.
12 I have nothing but the highest praise for the Augustinian Sisters at Boarbank Hall at Grange-over-Sands. Their prayers and pastoral support helped me enormously.
13 Archimandrite Sophrony, *On Prayer* (St Vladimir's Seminary Press, 1998), p. 84.
14 Andrew Clitherow, *Into Your Hands* (SPCK, 2001), pp. 40–1.